Inclusion for Children with Dyspraxia/DCD

A Handbook for Teachers

Kate Ripley

David Fulton Publishers

London

David Fulton Publishers Ltd
2 Park Square, Milton Park, Abingdon, Oxon, OX14 4RN

www.fultonpublishers.co.uk

First published in Great Britain by David Fulton Publishers 2001
Reprinted 2003

Transferred to Digital Printing 2007

10 9 8 7 6 5 4 3 2

Note: The right of Kate Ripley to be identified as the author of this work has been asserted by her in accordance with the Copyright, Designs and Patents Act 1988.

British Library Cataloguing in Publication Data
A catalogue record for this book is available from the British Library.

ISBN 1-85346-762-6

Publisher's Note
The publisher has gone to, great lengths to ensure the quality of this reprint but points out that some imperfections in the original may be apparent

Typeset by FiSH Books, London

Contents

Acknowledgements

To: Tracy Mander for her patience with the changes to the manuscript; Charlotte Ripley for her illustrations; Peter Cartlidge for sharing the activities of the Esteem Club; and East Sussex County Psychology Service.

Also to CME: my muse.

Chapter 1

An Introduction to Praxis

Children who are identified as having difficulties with movement control are increasingly recognised as children with special educational needs. Some of these children will be at the extreme end of the normal distribution for motor skills: opposite to that of a Michael Owen/Denise Lewis and any of our other sporting icons. Others may have diagnosed medical conditions such as lax ligaments, low muscle tone or dyspraxia. Changes in attitude and understanding during the past decade have resulted in a new awareness of the effects that motor impairment may have on learning, self-esteem and social/emotional development.

These guidelines have been compiled to help teachers to understand more about the difficulties that children with motor-skill problems experience in school. The guidelines address the social implications as well as the associated learning difficulties and include some strategies to support children through the key stages.

Praxis

'Praxis' is a Greek word which is used to describe the learned ability to plan and to carry out sequences of coordinated movements in order to achieve an objective. 'Dys' is the Greek prefix 'bad' so dyspraxia literally means bad Praxis.

A child with difficulties in learning skills such as eating with a spoon, speaking clearly, doing up buttons, riding on a bike or handwriting may be described as dyspraxic. The movements which are involved in these activities are all skilled movements which are learned and voluntary, i.e. under the conscious control of the individual who carries them out.

Developmental Dyspraxia is found in children who have no significant difficulties when assessed using standard neurological examinations but who show signs of an impaired performance of skilled movements. Developmental Dyspraxia refers to difficulties which are associated with the development of coordination and the organisation of movement.

Praxis is learned behaviour but it also has a biological component. The sequence of motor development is predetermined by innate biological factors that occur across all social, cultural, ethnic and racial boundaries (Gallahue 1992), but the learning of motor skills can only progress in the context of continued interaction with the external environment. The early learning of movement skills usually takes place in the context of play.

Alternative terminology

The term 'Developmental Dyspraxia' has been selected as the title for the guidelines because dyspraxia has implications for the processing of sensory information as well as for the planning and execution of skilled voluntary movements. There are, however, four terms in common use to describe motor problems, particularly in the USA and Canada and these may appear in the reports from other professionals.

In 1994 the term 'Development Coordination Disorder' (DCD) appeared in the *Diagnostic and Statistical Manual of Mental Disorders* (DSM IV). The characteristics were described as:

- problems with movement and spatial-temporal organisation;
- qualitative differences in movements from peers;
- the presence of co-morbid features which affected a wide range of functioning.

Like Developmental Dyspraxia, the condition was seen as being a chronic, usually permanent, condition in which the impaired motor performance could not be explained by the age or the ability of the child in question. Polatajko *et al.* (1995) have described DCD as a problem with the execution of motor movements and it is often used synonymously with the term 'Clumsy Child Syndrome'.

For Sugden and Keogh (1990) a diagnosis of Developmental Dyspraxia should include, as a key feature, problems with the planning or conceptualising of motor acts.

The final term 'Sensory Integrative Dysfunction' places the emphasis on the ability to receive and to process information from the senses with accuracy.

There is, as yet, no common agreement about the groups of children (the population) that each of these terms describe (Polatajko *et al.* 1995). The term 'Developmental Dyspraxia' has been the one used in these guidelines because it includes reference to all the three elements which are needed for efficient Praxis.

Three elements, as described in the following sections, are needed for efficient Praxis and the term 'Developmental Dyspraxia' best relates to all three of these components. They are represented in Figure 1.1.

1. Sensory input and processing

Terms such as 'Sensory Integrative Dysfunction' emphasise the receiving of accurate information from the senses, particularly vision, tactile receptors, the vestibular apparatus and the proprioceptive system. The hearing, smell and taste receptors may be relatively less important in the context of Praxis as a child gets older.

Five senses (vision, hearing, smell, taste, touch) are familiar to all, but the vestibular and proprioceptive systems may require some further explanation.

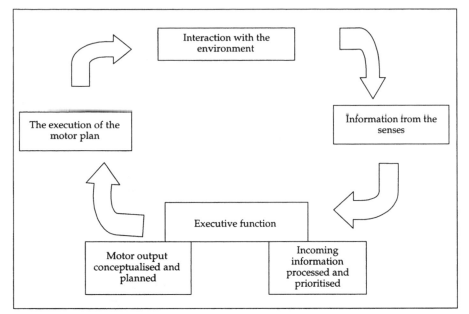

Figure 1.1 The components of efficient Praxis

The vestibular system

The vestibular receptors are found in the inner ear. The vestibular sense responds to body movement in space and changes in head position. It automatically coordinates the movements of eyes, head and body, is important in maintaining muscle control, coordinating the movements of the two sides of the body and maintaining an upright position relative to gravity.

The information from the vestibular apparatus is projected to the cerebellar area of the brain, which is associated with a range of functions.

Function	Possible difficulties
1. Learning new movements	Learning new skilled movements will be slower than for most children.
2. Memory for movement patterns	The movements that we learn slowly and then become automatic, like walking, driving, handwriting, may never achieve the degree of automaticity and, therefore, efficiency that other people achieve. Children may always have to think about the mechanics of handwriting, and use visual monitoring for each letter and word. Most adults can shut their eyes and write their name efficiently because the motor plan is well established.
3. Fluency of movements	Movements such as running or the transition between different

4. Sequencing of movements

movements may appear clumsy and dysfluent because the timing is faulty. Complex actions usually involve a whole sequence of movements which need to be assembled in the correct order, e.g. when performing a dance routine or changing gear in a car. Some people find sequences of movement very hard to achieve.

5. Control of posture

Children who find it hard to maintain a steady balance and posture may:

- fall frequently;
- lean against people or furniture when lining up, etc.;
- continually readjust their posture so that they may appear hyper-kinetic and can be misdiagnosed as AD/HD;
- find it especially hard to sit still for carpet time because their posture is unsupported;
- find it hard to maintain an upright trunk (upper body) to free their arms for writing and other activities.

The proprioceptive system

The proprioceptors are present in the muscles and joints of the body and give us an awareness of our body position. They enable us to guide arm or leg movements without having to monitor every action visually. Thus, proprioception enables us to do familiar actions such as fastening buttons without looking. When proprioception is working efficiently, adjustments are made continually to maintain posture and balance and to adjust to the environment, for example when walking over uneven ground.

The proprioceptive system helps us to develop a body image by giving information about where different parts of our body are positioned relative to the environment. Without a clear image of our own body boundaries, it is hard to develop a spatial awareness of our surroundings.

Children who have difficulties with proprioception may:

- find it hard to know where on their bodies they have been touched unless they have observed the movement;
- find it hard to identify objects that they could recognise visually in a 'feely bag' (or for adults, to get out the mobile telephone quickly from a large handbag);
- find it hard to build up the mini-motor plans which we rely on for fastening shoelaces, buttons, while our attention is engaged elsewhere;

- fall frequently in situations such as walking over rough ground or moving from one surface to another;
- show small adjustment movements, particularly of the limbs, in an unconscious attempt to stimulate the proprioceptors in order to get feedback about where parts of their body are in space. This, linked with other postural adjustments because of postural control difficulties, may increase the possibility of an inappropriate AD/HD diagnosis unless a full multidisciplinary assessment is carried out.

The information which has been received from all seven senses has to be interpreted by the brain. The ability to integrate the information from the senses is known as sensory integration. Occupational therapists will often start their treatment of a dyspraxic child by working on sensory input and sensory integration.

2. Motor planning

The second component of Praxis is the ability to plan a coordinated response which may involve movements and movement sequences which have a range of complexity. Children who have difficulties with this planning component have been identified as having Ideational Dyspraxia.

The term describes difficulties with the planning of a sequence of coordinated movements or with actions which involve the manipulation of objects. The individual actions may be carried out competently, e.g. hammering a wooden peg, but the order of the actions may be lost, e.g. failing to put the peg in the hole before hammering. In older children, organising tasks, equipment and their ideas may become a problem.

3. The execution of the motor plan

The third component of efficient Praxis is the execution of the motor plan. Difficulties in this area have been described as Ideo-motor Dyspraxia, and the terms 'DCD' or 'Clumsy Child Syndrome' emphasise this component of Dyspraxia. Children with Ideo-motor Dyspraxia know what they want to do, but find it hard to execute their action plan. The performance of individual actions may be clumsy, slow, awkward, non-fluent and children may experience particular problems with transition: moving from one action to the next. Everyone has experiences of failing to meet their own expectations about executing a motor plan, whether it is a poor putt or dropping the casserole dish. However, most of us manage a 'good enough' performance most of the time.

The development of Praxis

The development of Praxis is a complex process which involves changes in the neural networks in the brain (learning) so that information from the senses is integrated with the planning and execution of skilled movements in order to achieve increasingly complex goals.

As movement skills such as walking or driving become automatic they are no longer a focus for attention but are taken for granted, so that we easily forget the complex learning process that led to these skilled performances. We do become aware if something goes wrong in one of our own established patterns (we sprain our wrist and have to work out new ways of opening a jar), or when we work with children who have had difficulty in acquiring these complex, skilled movement sequences.

It is probably an exaggeration to describe babies as 'just a bundle of reflexes', but reflexes such as the suck reflex and the flexion reflex do play a large part in the early movement repertoire of a neonate. However, from the first time the baby turns its head towards a sound or a face or reaches to touch the breast, we begin to see the signs of voluntary movements developing. Movement development (like the development of language) is an example of maturationally controlled behaviour, but the sequence can only unfold by continually interacting with the physical environment. The characteristics of this kind of behaviour are listed below.

Maturationally controlled behaviour

- is pre-programmed to emerge at a particular stage if the environment is within normal limits;
- emerges before it is critically needed;
- requires some learning but it is not significantly speeded up by coaching;
- involves the unfolding of a regular sequence of events.

The process of development can be observed by 'babywatching' as babies learn to sit up, pull themselves upright, take their first steps hanging onto the furniture and eventually learn to walk independently without falling over or bumping into things (too often). Not all children learn to organise and control their voluntary movements at the same rate. Nor will they all develop to the same level of physical competence. If we study the population, most people will have average coordination, while smaller numbers have either very good or very poor skills. These individual differences are true of all biological variation and perhaps the most obvious one is height. The scientific way of describing the range of individual differences is by means of the 'normal curve' of distribution (see Figure 1.2).

The idea of a normal distribution of motor skills may create problems for an assessment of dyspraxia because it may be hard to decide whether a child should be considered to be dyspraxic or just relatively poorly coordinated. At an operational level, a motor-skills problem should be taken seriously if a child finds it difficult to carry out the motor activities which are usually expected for someone of that age and this causes distress to the child and the parents and affects access to the curriculum.

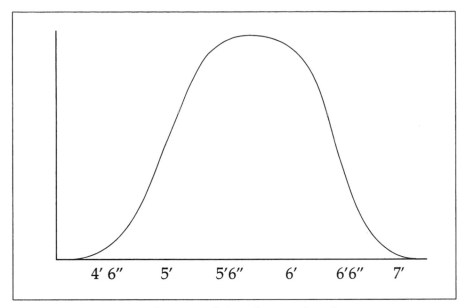

Figure 1.2 The normal curve of distribution: height

We may anticipate that some children will have a head start because of their genetic inheritance, while others may share a family difficulty with the development of Praxis.

L (see Case Study 1, p. 15) was the youngest of four boys, all of whom showed some signs of dyspraxia like their father, but L experienced the most difficulties in the family.

A simple scenario, shown below, will serve to illustrate some of the key components in the development of Praxis.

> One of the early toys that most babies have is the rattle that parents attach to the pram. A baby will respond to this novelty by showing general excitement which involves random movements of his arms and legs and even the whole body. The movement itself will cause the toy to vibrate and make a noise which in turn stimulates more interest in the toy. An accidental contact with the toy, as a result of the excited movements, will give pleasurable feedback in terms of noise and movement of the toy. In a relatively short time most babies learn how to strike the toy deliberately in order to get it to move and to make a noise. The action of the baby becomes more skilled over time.
>
> (Ripley *et al.* 1997)

What has the baby learned from this sequence of events?

1. The baby has begun to be able to move different parts of its body independently. This is an essential prelude to many everyday activities such as:

- being able to use one hand as a dominant hand and the other as a support hand in order to perform everyday activities like opening a box, crisp packet etc.;
- walking along while exercising other skills such as controlling the lawn mower;
- coordinating complex skills such as pedalling and steering a bike.

Children who are late to develop this aspect of control often show associated movements which disrupt the fluency of their movements and can make them look 'odd' to other children, e.g. flailing arms while running.

2. Visual-motor integration

In the case of the rattle, the baby is also learning to integrate information from the visual system in order to refine the motor plan. Recent studies involving brain imaging have suggested that the visual system has different networks which are involved in recognising faces (Bruce and Young 1986), or objects, and for linking in with the motor system. As babies interact with their environment, they appear to store in their memories the motor plan that they have used to interact with that object on previous occasions. We can test this out for ourselves when our visual 'plans' are fooled in some way (see Figure 1.3). If a light plastic brick which looks identical is substituted for a household brick, the force and effort involved to pick it up will be wrong.

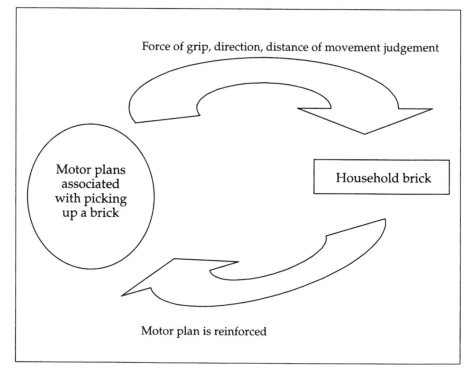

Figure 1.3 Picking up a household brick

In a recent TV series, *The Human Brain*, Professor Greenfield demonstrated how visual illusions can 'fool' the object recognition system but not the visual-motor system.

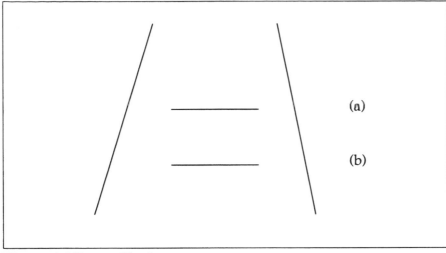

Figure 1.4 Ponzo illusion

In this illusion, the topmost horizontal line (a) looks longer than (b) to the object recognition system. However, it can be shown that the visual-motor system is not so easily fooled if the illusion is set up using wooden or plastic strips to represent (a) and (b). When someone is asked to pick up the strips, they use the same degree of finger thumb separation to pick up both strips.

Efficient links between the visual system, visual memory and learned motor plans are needed to achieve the visual-motor integration which helps us to control aspects of movement such as:

- force
- direction
- amplitude
- distance.

The precise control of the fine-motor movements which are needed to thread a needle, mend a watch or learn to write are heavily reliant on efficient visual-motor integration.

People who find it hard to control the force of movement may:

- hit someone when they intended a friendly gesture;
- smash the stem of a wine glass when they try to put it on the table, or smash the Lego model as they put in on the display table;
- find it hard to cut with a knife, or exert too much force so the food skids off the plate.

People who find it hard to control the amplitude of movement may:

- find it hard to pick up and place objects efficiently, e.g. doing peg patterns;
- knock over the glass of water when they go to pick it up.

People who find it hard to judge direction and distance may:

- find driving in traffic or crossing the road quite dangerous;
- not get out of the way of big children running towards them;
- find it particularly hard to deal with moving objects.

The basal ganglia of the brain is involved with the control of these aspects of movement together with the initiation and duration of movement.

Appendix I presents the timetable for the achievement of motor goals which is shown by most children.

The incidence of dyspraxia/DCD

The estimated incidence of dyspraxia/DCD in the population varies considerably and this reflects the lack of consensus in definitions and the range of diagnostic tools which may have been employed.

The reported prevalence varies between 5 per cent (Henderson and Hall 1982) to 19 per cent (Keogh 1968). As a guide, it has been suggested that about 1:10 children may experience coordination difficulties which will affect their performance of the activities expected at their age (Hoare and Larkin 1991).

As a developmental disorder, the prevalence of boys over girls would be expected for dyspraxia/DCD. This has been reported by many researchers – Gordon and McKinlay 1980, Henderson and Hall 1982, Keogh *et al.* 1979. However, a few studies have reported a more equal distribution between boys and girls (Gubbay 1975, Maeland 1992).

The assessment of Developmental Dyspraxia should include some information about all the aspects of functioning which are relevant to efficient Praxis in order to evaluate the difficulties which a child may experience both socially and educationally. A multidisciplinary assessment in which the teacher plays a key role is, therefore, the preferred model for assessment.

Chapter 2

The Assessment of Dyspraxia: A Team Approach

The evidence suggests that parents are usually the first to notice their children's difficulties but that it may be hard for them to get those initial concerns acknowledged by their health visitor, GP or visiting therapists. Some parents will actively seek a label for their child's difficulties, whereas others may be alarmed by the idea of a diagnostic label. Teachers and educational psychologists will be aware of the need to respect the sensitivity of parents.

What parents noticed as different may be tabulated as follows:

Area of difficulty	Percentage reported
Speech difficulties	50
Running	55
Jumping	52
Hopping	61
Late to develop a mature grasp	50
Balancing and bike-riding	68
Throwing and catching	90

(Chesson *et al.* 1991)

The evidence also suggests that children whose movement and coordination difficulties show themselves in speech may be identified more quickly than others and that they may be referred directly to a speech and language therapist before they start school. However, not all therapists will be aware of the other movement difficulties that a child might have, and a child may enter school with relatively clear speech but with other significant motor problems yet to be identified and assessed.

Children can be referred to the speech and language therapist from birth onwards and a dyspraxic child may have feeding difficulties which prompt a very early referral.

If verbal dyspraxia is suspected, the speech and language therapist will use a range of formal and informal tests to assess:

- oral skills;
- the speech sound system;
- the sequencing of sounds;
- the control of breathing and phonation (the production of sounds);

1. The contribution of parents

2. Assessment by the speech and language therapist

- prosodic features of speech (e.g. rate of production, rhythmic quality, pitch, intonation, nasal resonance, volume);
- dribbling.

A child may be described as having oral dyspraxia if he or she has difficulties controlling the lips, and/or tongue, or coordinating all the movements connected with swallowing. These are movements which involve the speech apparatus but the problems are evident before and independent of any attempts to speak.

Children with oral dyspraxia may show early difficulties with sucking, swallowing and chewing which can make mealtimes and trying new foods a source of stress for the child and family that persists over time. For many, but not all children, oral dyspraxia is associated with later speech problems.

Verbal dyspraxia, however, has consequences beyond the control of the speech apparatus itself so that the language system is also affected. Children with verbal dyspraxia may show difficulties with the organisation of the sound system of language (phonology) and with the organisation of their expressive language.

Verbal dyspraxia is frequently associated with a more generalised dyspraxia and the therapist would usually observe the child's movements in a range of settings and refer to other members of the assessment team, if appropriate.

Speech and language therapy assessment might include the elements shown below in Figure 2.1.

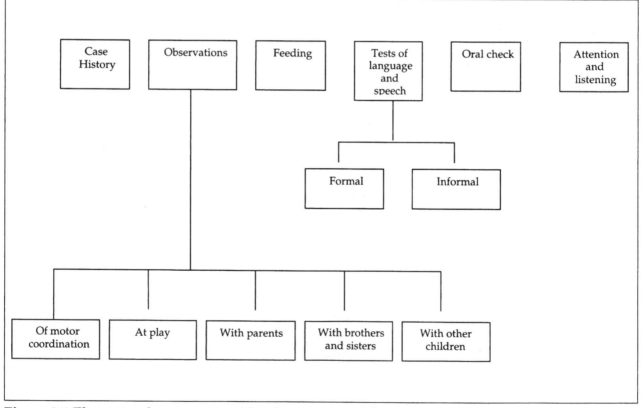

Figure 2.1 Elements of an assessment by the speech and language therapist

Referral to the occupational therapist is usually made via a medical route: a GP or school doctor; but some health trusts will accept referrals from other professionals including the SENCO in a school. The occupational therapist will consider the motor functioning relevant to all aspects of life including school, home and play. The occupational therapist may use a range of assessments both formal and informal which commonly include the following:

Assessment of Motor Impairment

- ABC of Movement
- The Bruininks-Oseretsky Test of Motor Proficiency
- Ayres' Clinical Observation of Neuro-behavioural and Neuro-muscular Functions.

Assessment of Sensory Perception and Integration

- Test of Visual Perceptual Skills
- Test of Visual Motor Integration (Beery 1989).

Assessment of Motor Function

- The Goodenough Harris Drawing Test
- The Jordan Left-right Reversal Test
- Handwriting Checklists.

3. Assessment by the occupational therapist

There is a wide range of medical conditions where symptoms can mirror those of dyspraxia. Each child should, therefore, have a comprehensive medical examination to look for signs of medical and neurological disease and epilepsy.

The paediatrician will look for an inability to carry out a sequence of voluntary movements effectively and a difficulty with motor planning. Discussion with parents will explore the developmental history, current problems such as attention control, and current motor skills which are appropriate to the age of the child. They may include writing, dressing, the use of cutlery, as well as the ability to ride a bike. Parents will also be asked about the birth history, past medical history, any developmental difficulties and the incidence of any similar difficulties within the immediate and extended family.

The paediatric examination will usually include a test of vision and hearing as well as a test of fine-motor skills and gross-motor skills. A full neurological assessment may also be undertaken. This is an assessment of physical function and will look at muscle tone, reflexes, range of movement, power, involuntary movements and sensations.

4. Assessment by the paediatrician

5. Assessment by the educational psychologist

The role of the educational psychologist is to work closely with parents, teachers, therapists and medical practitioners in order to:

- clarify the nature of the motor impairment;
- assess the implications for learning;
- assess the classroom as a learning environment for the child;
- assess the implications for access to the National Curriculum;
- identify the social, emotional and behavioural implications of the motor impairment.

Chesson *et al.* (1991) commented that although the educational psychologist had a key role in the identification of dyspraxia in children, few children in their study had been referred to the educational psychologist before starting school. They also found that more referrals to the occupational therapist were initiated by the educational psychologist than by any other professional group.

When school-age children are referred to the educational psychologist, motor skills are seldom identified as the main area of concern. An analysis of referrals indicates that teachers may express concerns about behaviour, learning or physical problems.

Behaviour

- The excluded, withdrawn child who is often apathetic, tearful, reluctant to attend school and has few friends.
- The 'naughty' child who may be a source of distraction in lessons, play the class clown and become aggressive when challenged.

Learning

- Slow progress because of task avoidance, a low rate of task completion, often called 'lazy' or poorly motivated, particularly if verbal skills are considered to be good.
- Untidy handwriting may be mentioned but this is not often linked to a specific avoidance of tasks which involve written output.
- Problems with drawing and visual perception may have been noted.
- Organisational problems may be identified as losing equipment and failing to do homework.

Physical problems

- Non-specific complaints about pains in head, abdomen and legs (often on days when PE is on the timetable).
- Nausea.
- Anxiety symptoms of bedwetting, eczema, asthma associated with particular demands at school or at home.

The first step is often to clarify the areas of difficulty which the child experiences.

CASE STUDY 1

L, Year 3

Initial concerns presented by his class teacher:

- anti-school, reluctant to come to school (parent);
- uncooperative, frequent refusal to attempt learning tasks (he often hides under the table);
- tearing up his own work and sometimes that of other children.

Strengths:

- likes listening to stories;
- joins in with class discussions and seems to have good general knowledge.

Discussion with his teacher and his mother suggested that L had difficulties with fine-motor skills which affected eating (a messy, fussy eater), dressing himself independently and, most significantly, the acquisition of writing skills. Observation confirmed that his task refusal was strongly linked to tasks which involved handwriting. Recording in some form occupies 40 per cent of the school day in the Juniors, according to the study of Leeds Primary Schools by Alexander (1992).

Most educational psychologists will use a range of strategies for the assessment of a child who presents with motor problems. These might include:

- a consultation model to collate information which is already available from parents, teachers and other sources;
- observations in a variety of educational and social settings;
- discussion with the child about their self-perception using projective techniques which are appropriate for the age of the child;
- checklists for teachers, parents or self-report which focus upon particular aspects of behaviour or learning;
- individual assessment in order to investigate specific areas of functioning in detail.

Once a child has started school, the class teacher and the SENCO will become key members of the multidisciplinary assessment team. Chapter 3 is devoted to their role.

6. The SENCO and class teacher

The Role of the Teacher in the Assessment of Developmental Dyspraxia

Once a child starts at school the teacher assumes a key role in monitoring progress towards developmental goals. A teacher with a group of four- to five-year-olds is often able to assess the motor competence of children when compared to their peers in a way which parents may not be in a position to do, particularly in the case of first children.

Chesson *et al.* (1991) found that of the 32 families in their study, the parents of 14 children were unaware that their child had difficulties before they started school. These children may have achieved their motor milestones for skills such as walking, sitting, grasp/release, feeding and eating rather later than most other children. They may have needed more practice to achieve a passable level of skill, but by the time they reached school age they had achieved 'good enough' levels of functioning in the familiar home environment.

Speech and language

About half the children who are later identified as having Developmental Dyspraxia have speech problems during their preschool years. Many of them will have been referred to the speech and language therapist and by the time they enter school their speech will be intelligible within context, even if in some cases it may sound a little immature. This passable level of speech and expressive language may mask real problems which only become apparent when the weak phonological (sound) system is put under pressure by the introduction of a phonic approach to reading, or when they fail to start to 'write' in sentences. It is often useful to ask the classroom assistant to record what they say 'verbatim' as well as 'tidying up' the early dictated sentences. This will then make it possible to monitor the development of a child's expressive language skills and provide valuable information on which to base the planning of an expressive language programme.

Preschool experience

Studies of children at playgroup suggest that children with Developmental Dyspraxia are slower to move around and explore their environment. If they do run off with the other children they quickly run out of energy because the effort which is involved in just moving about requires more stamina.

It is likely that they will have had less experience of activities such as climbing, swimming, balancing and using big apparatus because of this. They may have an awkward gait, particularly when running, and show associated or compensatory movements which make them look different from other children.

Difficulties with oral skills may have led to some fussy eating patterns, and problems with the coordination of chewing, swallowing or even getting food to their mouth accurately can make eating a messy business. Mealtimes may, therefore, have become quite tense for parents and their children. The feeding and eating difficulties which have been problematic at home may influence how the children feel about snack times or staying to school dinner.

Entry into school

The preschool experiences may, all too often, result in the child on entry to school being perceived by the other children as the one who can't:

- keep up in the playground;
- pedal and steer the bike;
- climb on the apparatus, jump off the apparatus or balance on the bench;
- dress or undress as independently as the others;
- cut, draw, stick;
- make models.

The attitude of teachers is crucial at this key time, as studies by Spence (1987) have shown that children quickly pick up and adopt the attitudes of their teachers. The more they hear a name in a negative context (*'Do hurry up, Johnny'*, *'Last again, Johnny'*, *'Do be careful, Johnny'*), the more likely they are to reject the child.

Entry to school presents a new set of challenges for the dyspraxic child and may expose a range of difficulties which were not so obvious during the Early Years. The demand for skilled, precise and coordinated movements of the hands and the eyes are particularly at a premium when a child is introduced to writing and reading.

Handwriting

During the early infant years, handwriting is the printing of individual shapes so that each letter is a drawn picture and each word is a collection of these individual pictures. A dyspraxic child may, with great effort, learn to copy these pictures, but the result is often larger and less uniform in size than for the others in the class. Lines which define the space may be useful once the letter forms are mastered, as a blank sheet of paper gives no cues about setting out the words. However, the lined paper should be specially prepared so that the spaces match the average letter size at that time. At Year 3 a child may be able to produce a few words which are printed neatly and may seem adequate if the time and effort which has been required to achieve this is not acknowledged.

The real problems with writing may not become apparent until the age of about seven when most writers learn a cursive (joined) script and begin to transfer the control of the writing of familiar words to automatic, proprioceptive control. (Test this out by closing your eyes and writing your name and address without looking.) As mature writers, a proprioceptive memory is established for high-frequency words so that vision is only used to organise the task and check the outcomes. A dyspraxic child will struggle to establish the automaticity of writing which comes when a mature pattern is established, and this will affect the speed of writing because the eye is not only doing its normal job of organising and evaluating what is written, but also checking on the hand movements. Even when visual checking is done, the result may appear 'untidy' or 'messy' because of proprioceptive confusions about direction and because of non-standard letter formation.

Achieving speed and legibility may become a challenge for both the child and the teacher so that specific teaching and the use of alternative means of recording, when content is the focus of the task, may be advisable.

Reading

A study by Chesson *et al.* (1991) demonstrated that of 32 children who had been referred for occupational therapy, and had had the usual screening procedures for their vision, 23 had problems with visual tracking and others with binocular control. For many children, ocular-motor problems may not become apparent until they start to learn to read.

Ocular-motor Dyspraxia is clinically identified when a person experiences difficulties moving their eyes independently without moving their heads. However, some dyspraxic children may show a range of difficulties which are associated with the control of eye movements.

Many dyspraxic children do read well but for others there may be problems associated with ocular control.

For some children, ocular-motor problems will affect their progress with reading and an early referral to an ophthalmologist may be appropriate. Some high street opticians in most towns will test dynamic binocular vision as well as carrying out tests of acuity for each eye. Children who experience these difficulties are often helped by carrying out simple eye exercises, and these can have quite significant effects upon their reading scores on conventional tests as shown in the Reading Age records for some of the 17 children studied by Bedwell and Ripley (1987).

The behavioural signs of ocular-motor difficulties may be observed in the dyspraxic 'at risk' population (Figure 3.1).

CASE STUDY 2

J, Year 4

When J was nine, his mother commented in her contribution to his statement of educational needs:

> He does find the physical act of reading very difficult. His silent reading is better than his reading aloud, but he has difficulty with sustained reading and often loses the meaning in a small print book. He was given glasses with the left eye occluded to help him develop a fixed reference eye and these have helped his attention span and concentration as long as he is reading a large print book. He may have exercises later to help improve his fixation on letters; due to his eye problems letters seem to swim.

> J had made a promising initial start with reading when he was presented with single words or a limited number of large words printed on each page. His problems became apparent as the print size decreased: there were more words on the page and he was expected to read for longer periods of time. Typically, children like J may frequently lose their place on the page and need to use a card to define each line for much longer than their classmates.

The Behavioural Signs Associated with Ocular-motor Problems

Ocular-motor problems may affect progress with reading. The behavioural signs include:

- slow progress with reading in an otherwise able child;
- a reluctance to read more than a few lines;
- an unexpected reluctance to read when the child reaches a stage in the reading scheme where the print size is reduced;
- a reluctance to choose books with small print or many lines on a page;
- missing words or missing lines when reading aloud;
- looking up at regular intervals and fixating on distant objects. This may be misconstrued as a lack of attention;
- rubbing the eyes after reading for a variable length of time and/or head shaking or other 'tic'-like movements;
- screwing up one eye or occluding one eye;
- an asymmetrical posture when reading and writing;
- watering or red eyes after reading for a variable length of time.

A child should show more than half of the signs on a regular basis before there is a cause for concern.

Figure 3.1 Signs in the dyspraxic 'at risk' population

Teacher observations

As children move about the classroom or the playground and attempt their work assignments, it is difficult for a teacher not to become aware of unusual movement patterns. Observation of a child may indicate that there are difficulties with fine- and/or gross-motor control.

Children with fine-motor problems may show some of the following features:

- a tendency to avoid practical tasks, possibly with immature grasp and release control;
- difficulty when attempting to use scissors and other classroom equipment;
- poor individual finger skills which may affect dressing and other self-help skills;
- difficulty in crossing the mid-line of the body and uncertain hand dominance beyond the age of seven years;
- delay in establishing a lead and support role for hands when attempting two-handed activities. This may affect skills such as eating using cutlery and early learning tasks such as threading;
- late development of a pincer grip in preparation for correct pencil grip;
- difficulty in naming left and right;
- poor pencil control when drawing and writing;
- speech problems and difficulties with oral skills.

A few children may show some misleading behaviour such as seeking out the construction toys in Year 2. In a developmental context they may be practising and enjoying these toys at a later stage in their development than usual. Their peers may have played with those Lego blocks, mastered the skills and moved on in their play.

Children with gross-motor problems may show some of the following features:

- reduced ability to maintain body posture resulting in a tendency to lean against things when standing and an inability to maintain body stillness. The appearance of over-activity and impulsivity may lead to confusion with AD/HD;
- lack of stamina, inability to walk long distances or keep up with action games;
- general lethargy, slow, ponderous response to instructions and task completion;
- poor muscle tone, 'floppy' movements or excessive tension and inability to relax;
- inability to change direction without overbalancing and a lack of precision when stopping or starting;
- limited spatial awareness, a tendency to bump into people and objects in the classroom;
- difficulty in estimating speed, distance and direction;
- inability to carry out a sequence of movements for PE or dance routines;
- poor sense of rhythm and timing, jerky movements;
- general disorganisation, never knowing where they should be or what they should be doing.

More detailed observation checklists for motor skills can be found in Appendix V.

If, as a teacher, you do become concerned about a child, a more systematic observation may be appropriate. The following checklists (pp. 23–5) for gross-motor, fine-motor and self-help skills were first compiled as part of an LEA screening programme (Ripley and Meades 1988), and have recently been adapted for use with children who are moving to Key Stage 2. The checklists were designed to be completed by observing how a child responds to everyday activities in the classroom or on the playground. The information from the checklists might then be used for a referral to the educational psychologist or the occupational therapist.

A standardised checklist, *The Movement Assessment Battery for Children* (MABC), is based on *The ABC of Movement* (Henderson and Sugden 1992) and is available for teachers to use. This provides a useful framework for the analysis of a child's movement difficulties and for deciding whether a full assessment using *The ABC of Movement* is indicated (see Figure 3.2).

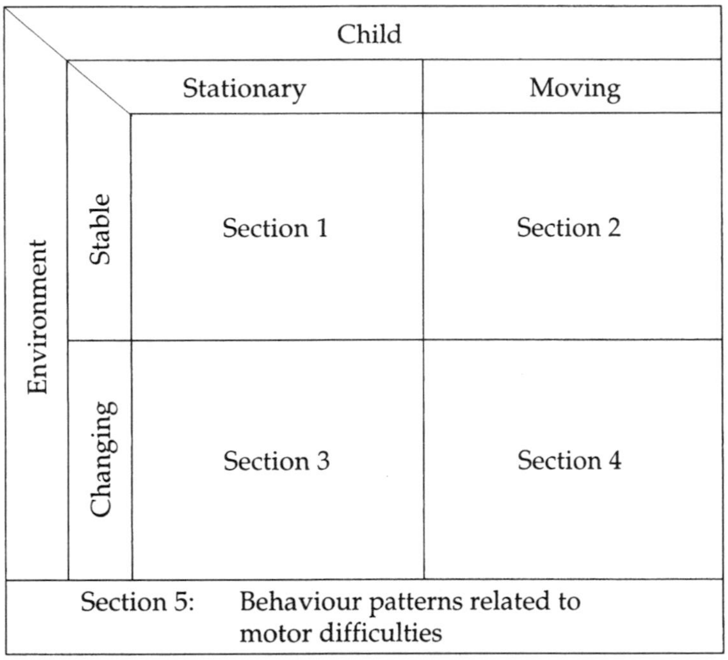

Henderson, S. E. and Sugden, D. A. (1992) *Movement Assessment Battery for Children; The Movement ABC Manual* Kent: The Psychological Corporation.

Figure 3.2 The framework for the analysis of movement: The Checklist Classification

In order to assess a child's motor skills using *The Movement Assessment Battery for Children* (MABC) a teacher would have to carry out observations in all four of the contextual settings. It is important, therefore, for the observation to take place in both the classroom and during physical activity sessions. Wright *et al.* (1994) found that the identification of children was more efficient when both class teachers and PE teachers completed the checklists, if the child did not have the same teacher for PE and games.

In a study of the effectiveness of the MABC for the identification of DCD, Pick and Edwards (1997), found that PE teachers were able to identify 47 per cent of the children, whereas teachers who only saw the children in class identified 25 per cent. The rates for the identification of the clumsy children were higher when the scores for individual sections were analysed, so a low score on one section may be evidence in itself of a child at risk for motor-coordination difficulties.

Conclusions

In the past, the impact of motor skill impairment upon the learning and social, emotional development of children has often been underestimated and even ignored. Once children start school, teachers are in the front line for identifying children at risk and putting into place interventions which will both help children to develop their motor skills and to find strategies which will reduce the personal and academic consequences of their poor motor skills.

Gross-Motor Skills: Observation Checklist

Key Stage 2

School: _____   NC Year: _____

Name of Child: _____   CA: _____   Date: _____

These activities should be incorporated into a PE lesson.

Can (s)he	Yes	No	Comments
1. stand on one leg (either leg) for 3–5 seconds?			
2. walk on tip-toe for 4m+? stand still on tip-toe?			
3. hop on either foot, 6+ times?			
4. skip using alternative legs for 5m+?			
5. control the speed of movement and change direction promptly on a signal?			
6. climb a ladder/rope ladder?			
7. leap over obstacles on or near the ground and jump off apparatus?			
8. copy sequences of movements which have been demonstrated?			
9. catch a ball, watching it carefully and prepare hands to receive it?			
10. throw, controlling both force and direction?			
11. run to kick a stationary ball towards a target, or kick a moving ball?			
12. lie still in a prone position for 30 seconds?			
Is the child rejected during group activities in PE?			
General observations about the quality of movement, e.g. awkward gait, compensatory movements (arm flapping when running), muscle tone (tense or 'floppy').			

Fine-Motor Skills: Observation Checklist

Key Stage 2

School: _____   **NC Year:** _____

Name of Child: _____   **CA:** _____   **Date:** _____

Can (s)he	Yes	No	Comments
1. fit together simple jigsaw puzzles (25 pieces +) and assemble construction toys?			
2. do up and undo easily accessible fastenings, e.g. zips, Velcro, large buttons?			
3. hold a pencil correctly?			
4. control pencil, crayons or paintbrushes well enough to produce recognisable pictures?			
5. draw a circle, square, triangle and diamond shape accurately?			
6. draw between lines (mazes) and trace over lines and dots?			
7. use scissors to cut out around a simple shape?			
8. manage a range of manipulative actions, e.g. unscrew a lid, thread beads, fill a container to a given level, use a handle to open and close a door?			
9. build a tower of ten bricks (attempt several sizes)?			
10. touch each finger with the thumb of the same hand (check both hands)?			
Has the child developed: a dominant hand? a support hand?			
General observations, reasons for concern about motor development, etc.			

Self-Help Skills: Observation Checklist

Key Stage 2

School: _____   **NC Year:** _____

Name of Child: _____   **CA:** _____   **Date:** _____

Can (s)he	Yes	No	Comments
1. manage the toilet without help?			
2. wash hands adequately after messy activities?			
3. dress/undress at the same speed as the others in the group?			
4. put on clothing in the correct order, orientation with a tidy(ish) result?			
5. manage fastenings, such as Velcro, large buttons, zips?			
6. keep track of personal possessions?			
7. collect the materials needed for a task with minimal help?			
8. move around the classroom without falling or bumping into children and furniture?			
9. navigate around the school?			
10. is she or he particularly accident prone in the playground.			

Chapter 4

The Social and Emotional Implications of Dyspraxia

To adults who have neither experienced dyspraxia (DCD) for themselves nor had close contact with children who have significant motor problems, this chapter may appear to have a negative focus. For those people who have 'lived with' significant levels of dyspraxia (DCD) there will be no surprises.

Motor skills within the normal population show a wide range of variability from world class athletes to people who see themselves as 'hopeless at tennis'. However, most people do develop a degree of motor competence that means they can get by in most situations without making fools of themselves by spilling things at the table, tripping over or dropping things and thereby embarrassing their friends and family. For children who have a clinical diagnosis of dyspraxia (DCD), their motor difficulties interfere with the way in which they are able to carry out the normal activities expected for a child of their age. The degree to which they are affected will range from the clumsy end of the normal distribution to a significant degree of impairment which affects daily life skills as well as learning. There is no simple one-to-one correspondence between the degree of motor difficulty and the social, emotional impact of the condition. However, the research evidence does indicate that children, and adults, who are perceived as 'clumsy' are at risk for a range of social, emotional and behavioural problems. The intention of this chapter is to promote an awareness of these risks and, thereby, change our perceptions about the children who are affected.

Historically, clumsy children have not been perceived sympathetically by their peers or even by adults. As early as 1937, Orton found that children who were slow in reaching their developmental goals for movement or were poorly coordinated were at risk of being described as lazy, careless or of low ability. Not much had changed over time when Walton (1962 cited in McGrath 1998) also found that clumsy children were described as lazy, badly behaved and 'mentally dull'. As our self-esteem is built up from how we are perceived by others, it is not surprising that Orton (1937) and Henderson (1993) commented on the low self-esteem of clumsy children.

Behaviour problems are often reported by teachers, and research has confirmed that children who have coordination problems frequently attempt to cover up their difficulties by 'exhibiting disruptive behaviour' (Kalverboer *et al.* 1993) or playing the 'clown' (Keogh *et al.* 1979).

CASE STUDY 3

Z, Year 3

Z was the son of an occupational therapist. His teacher perceived him as a naughty boy who disrupted the class by playing the fool. An example of this behaviour was cited as his clowning while the class were learning the country dance for May Day (i.e. a sequence of coordinated movements). Even when his teacher had watched the administration of *The ABC of Movement*, it was difficult for her to see him as a boy who 'can't' rather than one who 'won't'.

'Playing the clown' is not the exclusive province of children in response to new motor challenges. An adult who had listened to the anecdote about Z, gave a personal account of her experience at an aerobics class. It was her first time and, when she realised that she was out of sequence, going the 'wrong' way and generally showing herself up, she began to play the clown. It took some minutes for her fully to realise what she was doing!

Although some children may act out their difficulties, others have been shown to have *high levels of anxiety*. The anxiety may be accompanied by symptoms of non-organic pain (Mellor 1980) such as the familiar tummy aches on PE days. Smyth (1992 cited in McGrath 1998) reported a range of emotional problems among children with coordination problems. These include:

- feelings of incompetence and inadequacy;
- depression;
- frustration which could lead to hostile, aggressive behaviour;
- mood swings.

Relationships with peers

We are all aware that positive relationships with peers are important for emotional, social and behavioural adjustment and wellbeing. There is a wealth of evidence which indicates that children with motor impairments are not popular among their peers:

1. McGrath (1998) studied 23 children who had poor coordination:
   22 of the 23 were rejected by their peers;
   Only one had a positive reputation;
   12 had an aggressive/disruptive reputation;
   10 had a sensitive/isolated reputation.
2. Gordon and McKinley (1980) also reported clumsy children as unpopular and figures of fun. The children are also at risk for being bullied at school as first documented by Olveus (1978) and subsequently confirmed by Losse *et al.* (1991) and Treanor (1994).

Why are peer relationships a problem?

Communication skills and physical skills both appear to be implicated in the problems which the children experience with peer relationships.

1. Verbal communication

About 50 per cent of dyspraxic children will experience early speech problems which may affect their relationships with peers even at playgroup. As Hadley and Rice (1991) stated 'Preschoolers behave as if they know who talks well and who doesn't and they prefer to interact with those who do.' Reduced intelligibility and poor grammar were found to be the most important factors in the failure of interactions among a preschool population. Children who interact less with their peers have fewer opportunities to practise their social skills and this can then compound the original problem.

Children who are unable to understand what is asked of them and/or are unable to make their needs and wishes known are at risk of becoming frustrated and throwing tantrums. Such children will also use physical means to interact with their peers for longer because they are unable to ask for a turn and 'negotiate' verbally. They may quickly be perceived as aggressive and or uncooperative by both peers and adults (Baker and Cantwell 1987).

CASE STUDY 4

D, Preschool

For some children the inability to understand or make their needs known can be temporary but they neatly illustrate the difficulties that less fortunate children experience.

D arrived in a Sussex playgroup as a Welsh-speaking child. He was large for his age and quickly learned that he could use his strength to take toys from other children. Within the first two weeks, D's mother had been summoned to discuss her aggressive child with the supervisor. D was an able boy who rapidly learned to communicate in English and so no longer needed to use physical methods to have his needs met. Now, well into his teens, he is perceived by all his teachers and peers as an unaggressive, gentle young man.

---

2. Non-verbal communication

Facial expression requires the coordination of many different muscle groups, and some dyspraxic children can present with blank, expressionless faces which give little feedback to other people. Teachers may comment:

- 'He is an unresponsive child, he just looks blank when I talk to him.'
- 'I never know if he has understood what I am telling him.'
- 'He never seems to get excited or enthusiastic about what we are doing.'

The ability to signal how you feel to other people is an important feature of non-verbal communication and the ability to 'signal' is closely linked to the ability to 'read' the expressions of other people. At playgroup, children who have these skills are more popular among their peers (Walden and Field 1990, Spence 1987).

It is not always immediately obvious, even to adults, why they feel uncomfortable when they attempt to interact with a person who does not signal their responses to what is said or done by using facial expression. As teachers we rely on feedback from our 'audience' to know whether we have been understood and how our message is being received. Without this feedback we quickly feel that we are failing to motivate the child or, to save our own self-esteem, may construe that the child is poorly motivated.

Dodge (1996) has explained this reaction in terms of a social information processing theory. As humans, we rely on the giving and receiving of appropriate social signals to guide our behaviour during our interactions with others. If the information we receive is limited, then we are less certain about how we might respond. A simple example may serve to illustrate the theory:

Johnny is playing on his own in the sand tray. Jane comes up and asks if she can play too. Johnny turns to her with a blank expression on his face. If Johnny smiles at her, Jane will know that she is welcome to join him. If Johnny frowns and says, 'Push off!' she may feel angry but at least her courses of action are clear. She may choose to walk away or to pick a fight. Johnny's 'blank' expression leaves Jane in limbo, uncertain about what course of action she should take. This feeling of uncertainty is the least rewarding state for Jane, and she is unlikely to approach Johnny again to ask if she can play.

3. Physical skills

In the Early Years, children with motor problems are slower to explore their environment and may fail to keep up with other toddlers because of their lack of stamina. Other children will notice differences of gait and limited competence during play – on the apparatus, on the bikes, etc. At school entry such a child may be identified as the one who: can't dress and undress as quickly as they can; is a messy eater they do not want to sit by, and is no good at drawing, glueing, cutting or model making. The teacher's reaction is crucial at this point. Spence (1987) discusses how young children adopt the attitudes of their teachers towards fellow classmates. If they often hear, 'Do hurry up, Johnny', 'Oh Johnny, do be careful', etc. they will learn to think negatively about Johnny themselves. In fact exhortations to 'try harder' or 'hurry up' usually only serve to exaggerate inept motor patterns.

Shoemaker and Kalverboer (1994) found that, by the age of six to seven, children with motor problems had low self-esteem and rated themselves less competent both physically and socially than they were rated by objective observers.

Proficiency in motor skills is important for status and popularity within the peer group (McGrath 1998), more important than either academic skills (Master 1982) or social competence (Boivin and Beguin 1989).

Children who experience motor difficulties are, therefore, at risk for being relatively unpopular among their peers. This is a process which may well have begun before they start school and, unless the issues are addressed, low status and social isolation may become entrenched within the group, see Figure 4.1.

The children who are caught in this negative loop will have great difficulty changing their position within the peer group without the active intervention of adults who are sensitive to their difficulties.

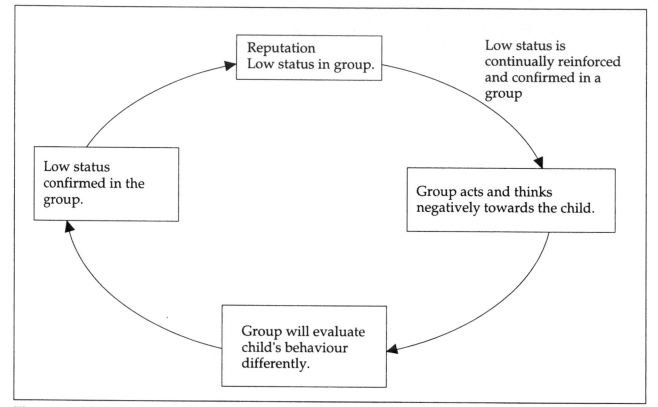

Figure 4.1 The process of becoming unpopular (see also Rogosch and Newcombe 1989, Hymel *et al.* 1990 and Coie 1990, all cited in McGrath 1998)

Strategies which may help to support children with motor impairment

- Support for children to develop friendships using standard techniques which are current in most schools:
    (a) circle time for the class, addressing issues of friendship;
    (b) circle of friends;
    (c) a buddy system.
- Social skill training in specific areas such as:
    (a) proxemics – the ability to recognise and maintain a comfortable, i.e. social distance when interacting with others;
    (b) mirror work to develop facial expression which reflects their mood.
- Record and plan the things that the child is able to do as successfully as others in the group and plan opportunities for these to be seen, praised and acknowledged by peers. It is important to remember that 'over the top' praise may be rejected by children with low self-esteem so the praise should be realistic and appropriate.

- With the help of parents, identify areas of strength and provide opportunities for these to be used in the classroom.
- In group work, assign roles so that the child can use his/her skills such as reading and avoid areas of difficulty such as the recording of information.
- Make modifications to the learning environment which are designed to reduce frustration and provide experiences of success – as discussed in Chapters 5 and 6.
- Teach motor skills through groups such as the 'Esteem Clubs' described in Chapter 8.
- Acknowledge that some difficult behaviour may be the result of frustration, e.g. a temper tantrum while changing for PE; reluctance to settle to a writing task and hostility when held to account. Address the problem rather than blame the child.
- Be aware that high levels of anxiety may be triggered by any physical challenges and that 'physical symptoms' may be the reaction. Handle these situations in a sensitive way and try to offer some options and choices which are appropriate to the child's level of skill in lessons such as games or PE.
- Difficulties with controlling the force and direction of movement can sometimes result in misunderstandings, especially on the playground. These need to be managed sensitively with reference to the dyspraxic problems of the students involved. For example:

  1. J insisted that all he had done was ask A to play with him. The LSA reported that he had hit A on the side of his face and A had retaliated.

     J's intention had been to attract A's attention by tapping him on the shoulder, but poor control of the force and direction of movement had determined the rest of the scenario.
  2. B was a teenager who had been verbally, and sometimes physically, bullied through his school career. Teachers at his secondary school had been aware and had put some strategies in place to protect him as well as addressing the bullying itself. One day, quite out of character, B lashed out at a classmate and hurt him quite badly. B was suspended from school.

     B's intention had been to stop the boy from teasing him. He lacked experience of the usual rough and tumble play which helps children to understand how much force is needed to make a point without doing serious damage. Children play-fight in much the same way as other young mammals, to establish dominance and the 'how much force' rules. Dyspraxic children may miss out on these early experiences.

When these types of difficulties are identified, children can be helped by working directly on the issues of force of movement. They may be encouraged:

- to pick up and move different objects;
- to carry out delicate movements and strong movements in physical exercises (see Chapter 8);
- to practise some elements of physical play, e.g. push and pull games;
- to discuss and practise ways of getting attention from peers in a more acceptable way.

CASE STUDY 5

A cautionary tale

M, Year 9

M had a history of behaviour problems at his primary school and had the involvement of the behaviour support team but their support was withdrawn in Year 9 because M was unwilling to cooperate. He was on the brink of exclusion when the educational psychologist was asked to attend a Pastoral Support Plan (PSP) meeting.

Assessment indicated that M had non-verbal reasoning skills at 99th centile but that his language skills were compromised (6th centile), especially in the area of the abstract, decontextualised language which is used as the main medium for teaching and learning. His social communication skills were not a problem and he used these to good negative effect with teachers and peers. He was perceived as a boy who was not very able.

Apart from his language problems, M was found to have additional difficulties with:

- Reading – 2nd centile, RA 8 yrs 0 months
  Some of his reading problems could be linked to the language difficulties, but he also experienced some ocular-motor problems such as:
  - difficulties with convergence (he said he had found eye exercises uncomfortable);
  - watering eyes when he attempted to sustain reading;
  - difficulty reading small print.

- Handwriting
  M was found to have significant problems with the mechanics of handwriting.
  - Age-equivalent score of 6 yrs 10 months.
  - Average writing speed of 13 wpm with uneven letter formation, variable gaps between words, not writing on lines.
  - His writing was barely legible, often judged untidy and needing to be done again.
  - M was left-handed so that his hand obscured what he had written and made it hard for him to proof-read, check spellings, etc.
  - He easily lost his place when attempting to copy from a text, worksheet or board (eye movement control implicated).
  - He found it hard to keep pace when note taking.
  - He found it hard to complete tasks within a time limit.

M may well have developed behaviour problems in school over time, but his frustration as a boy with well above average non-verbal reasoning skills who found it hard to use language as a medium for learning, read fluently and write efficiently, had undoubtedly contributed to his untenable situation in Year 9.

Chapter 5

Key Issues for Key Stages 1 and 2

There are some general considerations which are relevant throughout a child's educational career and others which are more pertinent at different key stages. The maintenance and enhancement of self-esteem will be relevant to all the key stages and there are four main additional challenges for a dyspraxic child in Key Stages 1 and 2:

- effective communication;
- handwriting and setting out work;
- reading;
- organisational skills.

Verbal communication

The research evidence suggests that about 50 per cent of children who are identified as dyspraxic will have some oral and/or verbal dyspraxia as a component of their motor profile. Fortunately, many children whose speech is difficult to understand are referred to the speech and language therapist before they start school. A good response to early intervention may help them to enter school with intelligible, if immature, speech which is adequate to communicate their needs and for them to interact socially with their peers. However, Early Years teachers do need to be aware of the history of such children because:

- there may be immaturities in their sound system (phonology) which would affect their response to a phonic approach to reading and spelling;
- there may be grammatical immaturities which will affect their ability to speak in sentences and, therefore, to generate grammatical sentences for writing. These immaturities can be identified and used as teaching targets if the scribe for their early 'writing' records verbatim what the child says as well as producing the 'tidied up' version of the sentence.

For some children, there may still be significant problems with both intelligibility and the organisation of expressive language which generate issues about how the teacher and other adults in school communicate effectively with the child. These children will benefit from ongoing support from the speech and language therapist.

Effective communication

Joint consideration may need to be given to:

- signing or other alternative means of communication;
- how the child communicates basic requests, e.g. asking for the toilet, going out to play, how to say 'yes' and 'no';
- the child's level of understanding;
- how the work undertaken by the speech and language therapist can be integrated with the programme in school and with the curriculum;
- when the child should be corrected, and the strategies which might be helpful, e.g. modelling;
- what effect the language problem is predicted to have on written language, reading, spelling and writing;
- decisions about at what stage specialist schemes such as 'Language through Reading' will need to be considered.

The language of the classroom

Teachers will need to be aware of the level of language which they habitually use for instructions, explanations and other verbal exchanges in the classroom. This is relevant for any child who experiences language problems and not only for children identified as having oral-verbal dyspraxia.

Specific teaching targets might include:

- The language associated with general classroom organisation: the sequence of events in the day or the sequencing of a task. Visual representations are always there for reference and do not fade like the spoken word, so visual timetables, cue cards and flow diagrams are all useful.
- Children should be taught the specific vocabulary needed for the following activities: lining up, circle time, PE, music and movement, maths, project work and organised games. Vocabulary which involves the concepts of space and time may be particularly confusing for children with dyspraxia.
- The speech and language therapist will help to assess the language profile of the child, their receptive as well as their expressive language skills. The class teacher is the one who is aware of the curriculum context and the language demands of the classroom, so the most effective way of supporting a child is by working together.

Children who have oral-verbal dyspraxia may have difficulties with receptive language skills which are independent of any problems with expressive language. These children will require the support strategies that are appropriate for any other child who has receptive language problems. However, understanding the language of spatial organisation, sequencing and time concepts may pose specific challenges for these children. This vocabulary may need to be specifically taught so that the child understands the 'technical', precise meaning of the words as well as any social usage which they may already know. For example, 'more' may be understood in the context of 'more beans' or 'more tickles' but not in the context of contrasts more/less or as part of a mathematical sequence of 'one more', 'two more', etc. The children may also have problems with other types of contrasts which involve movement or spatial awareness, for example push/pull, front/back, left/right.

The teaching of this key vocabulary can usefully follow the sequence of:

1. Teaching the concept in a structured setting, possibly one-to-one for some children.
2. Planning small-group activities which target the vocabulary which is to be generalised, e.g. *next to, behind, in front of,* using small world play items or game activities which involve the movement of children in space.
3. Targeting the use of the vocabulary in the context of the classroom and the curriculum, e.g. '*next to*' when lining up or during PE, '*one more/one less*' in the context of number work.

The most common difficulty experienced by children who have oral-verbal dyspraxia is with expressive language skills. The effects may have an impact at the level of:

- the organisation of the child's sound system, phonology;
- the accurate production of individual sounds or clusters of sounds (e.g. <u>str</u> ing);
- the sequencing of sounds or syllables within words (e.g. aminal);
- the sequencing of words in sentences;
- the organisation of expressive language itself through the sequencing of ideas within paragraphs or for an extended writing assignment.

These difficulties may affect educational attainments, e.g. learning to read using a phonic approach if the phonological system is insecure, or attempting to compose a sentence for the LSA to scribe in the early stages of free writing. The verbatim recording of what a child says in this context will provide valuable information about language-learning targets which may be relevant for the child, e.g. '*We goed out*' would indicate that work on irregular past tenses would be useful.

The strategies which are helpful to address these difficulties are discussed in detail in *Inclusion for Children with Speech and Language Impairment* (Ripley *et al.* 2001), and are beyond the scope of this handbook.

Nevertheless, it is important for teachers to be aware of these potential difficulties and to consider their impact on accessing the curriculum and on participation in group activities. Children who are uncertain that they will be understood are less likely to volunteer information or respond to questions in a group setting than their peers. They may also need time to organise their expressive language in order to make a response, and it may be difficult for any teacher in whole-class settings to give them the time they need without other eager children offering contributions for them. Some pre-preparation by a classroom assistant of the vocabulary and some responses to agreed questions may help the children to take a more active role in such discussions.

Difficulties with *volume control* and *prosody* may make some children with oral-verbal dyspraxia sound different when they do talk. Breath control, voice monitoring and awareness of the spatial or acoustic features of the environment are all linked to our ability to adapt the volume of our voices to the context of a conversation. Some children with oral-verbal dyspraxia may appear always to be shouting, even if they are communicating sensitive information in close proximity to the listener. Their attempts to 'whisper' to a neighbour may disturb the whole group. Others may struggle to produce sufficient volume to be heard, especially in group situations.

For other children, prosody may be an issue. This means that they do not use the range of intonation patterns that contribute to the meaning of what we say. Their voices may sound monotonous and 'flat'. To understand the importance of prosody in communication, read the following variations on a sentence, putting the emphasis on the words in italics. Think about the subtle differences in meaning between the versions of the sentence.

I didn't say he hit me.
I *didn't* say he hit me.
I didn't *say* he hit me.
I didn't say *he* hit me.
I didn't say he *hit* me.
I didn't say he hit *me*.

Case Study 6 (Year 3, later in this chapter) and Case Study 12 (Year 1, Chapter 7) are examples of children who experience difficulties with volume control and prosody. The strategies which were used to help them to address these problems are described.

Strategies to facilitate communication in the classroom

- Use other children to help: they can often tell what the child has said.
- Do not ask for repetitions as you will probably get a different version.
- Use pictures or symbols as a resource to facilitate communication.
- Repetition and clarification can be undertaken so responsibility passes to the child, by picking out the words you have heard (or think you have heard) and feeding them back to the child. Keep listening for recognisable words and keep feeding them back before too much more is said. By using these strategies, the conversation has a better chance of being maintained and some responsibility is passed to the child for supporting the listener without the build-up of too much frustration.
- Use the home/school book to get information about what has happened, is happening and will happen in the child's life. It is usually easier to understand what is being said if you have a context.
- Encourage natural gestures, if a signing system is not being used.
- Encourage the use of non-verbal cues, to help the child maintain the sequence of information. This reduces loading on the brain by giving time to concentrate on speech production, sentence formulation, word selection and any other techniques suggested by the therapist that ought to be practised.
- Be positive: it helps build confidence and enables the child to become more effective at monitoring their own performance.

All of these strategies could be practised in games, play situations and social skills games and activities.

CASE STUDY 6

K, Year 3

Some children who have oral-verbal dyspraxia may have few problems with their sound system and expressive language which affect their ability to communicate effectively. They may, however, have difficulties with controlling the volume and intonation patterns of their speech production.

K had his hearing checked before he started school because he always spoke very loudly, using a voice which was also quite 'flat'. His loud voice could be an embarrassment when he went out with his family and frequently disturbed his classmates when the children were supposed to be working quietly.

1. K was allocated some sessions with an LSA
   * to use a tape recorder to practise a soft and a loud voice with immediate feedback of his voice;
   * to discuss when people use a loud voice and a soft voice;
   * to carry out shared reading of a familiar text with K being encouraged to use differences in volume and intonation patterns appropriate for the characters and events. The LSA modelled how to do this first and K began to use the 'voices' spontaneously over time;
   * some of the shared reading was tape-recorded so that K could hear his different voices and discuss whether he had whispered just like a little mouse etc.
2. K's teachers shared a secret signal with K which told him if he needed to reduce the volume of his speech.
3. K joined groups of children working on play scripts and recording their playlets on tape.
4. K's teacher introduced role plays as part of circle time. All the children were encouraged to be more aware of the volume and stress patterns in their speech and how this was interpreted by a listener. They practised cross voices, calm voices, etc. as a group.

Non-verbal communication

Some children with dyspraxia have problems signalling facial expression and may appear 'blank' or unresponsive in both facial expression and body language. This has been shown to have implications for:

* social relationships and social acceptance as discussed in Chapter 4;
* the ability to read the expressions of other people accurately.

Special social skill targets may be needed for such children in addition to the social skills training that many dyspraxic children require.

CASE STUDY 7

S, Year 5

S was brought to the attention of the educational psychologist primarily because of his difficulties with handwriting, although the SENCO had noted some other dyspraxic features when she observed him in the playground. Discussion with his class teacher indicated that S presented as an unresponsive boy who appeared passive and difficult to motivate. He was a good reader, but never seemed overtly enthusiastic about reading or any other activities. Further investigation suggested that he had difficulty signalling his mood using facial expression.

S was allocated some sessions with an LSA in school and his parents' support was enlisted to help generalise his programme into real-life situations. The programme included:

- mirror work on copying facial movements;
- mirror work on copying facial expressions which were linked to mood – starting with the basic 'happy', 'sad', and moving on to more subtle expressions;
- practice identifying facial expressions of other people, familiar and unfamiliar, from pictures;
- modelling facial expressions for others to guess, using the play exercises;
- specific targets – smile when you greet people:
  - practise the target with the LSA;
  - generalise to the teacher and peers in the classroom;
  - generalise to the community with the help of his parents.

Handwriting

Handwriting is a core goal for the Early Years and, in the UK, children are expected to start learning how to make individual letter shapes from an early age. In terms of their motor development, many children will find this quite difficult at first, but children with dyspraxia/DCD will continue to struggle with this skill for an indefinite period. The phases in the development of handwriting are led by the development of the motor skills which are a necessary prerequisite and are maturationally controlled. Problems associated with the control of the force and direction of movement may affect the ability of children with dyspraxia/DCD to:

- learn the letter patterns;
- hold the pencil with a grip that is neither too tight nor too loose;
- exert pressure on the paper which is sufficient without pressing too hard.

Learning letter patterns

In the early stages of learning to write, children are required to use an unjoined script, usually on a blank sheet of paper. At this stage for all children each letter is an individual picture, and in terms of their motor development they are not ready to join their script. All children can be helped by an adult verbalising the letter patterns as they model them.

Additionally, children who have delayed motor development may benefit from writing practice which is:

- large scale to ensure maximum kinaesthetic feedback from the hand and arm as well as from the fingers. (Early writing skills are from the shoulder movements for all children.);
- large scale to ensure maximum feedback of left-to-right progression;
- on a vertical surface so that up and down has meaning.

Once the patterns are established, the size can be reduced, the skill can be transferred to a sloping surface and the skills practised to fluency.

The developmental stages for the development of pencil control are summarised in Appendix II.

Writing posture

Some children who have dyspraxia/DCD find it hard to maintain the trunk stability which enables them to establish a sitting position which frees up their hands and arms in order to carry out table-top activities or writing. The best chance of achieving stable posture is when there is a three-point anchorage: bottom on the chair and two feet on the ground.

Children of course, come in different shapes and sizes but, unfortunately, classroom furniture is built around the idea of a standard child. It may be possible to adapt the furniture – blocks under desk and chair legs, add cushions and foot rests to ensure that children are as comfortable as possible before they start to write. Even children who have no motor-skill problems can suffer from muscle and joint strain if they are required to write for long periods in an uncomfortable position.

Pencil grip

Children are actively encouraged in most classrooms to adopt a tripod grip and this can be facilitated by the use of triangular pencils and other devices. The conventional tripod grip is flexible, but for some children who have motor delay it does not offer the stability which they need in order to control the pencil effectively. Children often find their own solutions, e.g. by putting more than one finger on the shaft of their pencil and a few, spontaneously, adopt what in table tennis is known as the 'penholder' grip (introduced into the sport by the Chinese International Team). For children who find it hard to control their pencil these alternative grips provide the necessary stability, even if some flexibility is lost.

Another aspect of grip is the force with which the pencil is held. A grip which is too loose will have the pencil sliding between the fingers so that the children are writing with their fingernails. A grip which is too tight puts stress on the fingers and hand so that children cannot write for any length of time. Some exercises to develop finger pressure are discussed in Chapter 8 and the local occupational therapy department will be able to provide warm-up exercises to develop finger control such as:

- *jogging:* moving the fingers individually up and down the pencil from tip to the end and back;
- *press ups:* bending and straightening the fingers while holding the pencil;
- *the aeroplane:* holding the pencil horizontally while rotating the wrist;
- *bending:* weaving the pencil held horizontally between the fingers.

A marker on the shaft of the pencil to indicate the 'grip zone' can be made simply by using coloured sticky tape for young children, whereas an elastic band wrapped round the shaft to stop 'grip slip' is more 'cool' for older children.

Pressure on the paper

Some children find it hard to exert sufficient force to make a mark on the paper; others exert a heavy pressure which is hard for them to sustain over time. The problem is related to the core difficulty with the control of the force of movement which is experienced by many dyspraxic children.

The device known as the 'carbon paper sandwich' (Figure 5.1) can help children to become more aware of the force of movement and how they can control that force. The same equipment can be used to shape up an increase or a decrease in pressure.

The transition to cursive script

In the middle phase of learning to handwrite, the control of the movement patterns changes from the arm/hand to the fingers and hand. This transition is often marked by a noticeable reduction in the size of the child's handwriting and usually occurs at about seven years of age.

This is about the time that a cursive (joined-up) script is introduced, and when teachers and parents become concerned about any enduring letter reversals.

Some children who have difficulties with motor-organisation struggle to learn the movement patterns for printed letters and they also may take longer to develop a cursive script. Traditionally, teachers have often left children who have problems with printing longer before introducing a cursive script. However, since the letter patterns are likely to take longer to become established, starting to join their writing at the same time as their peer group may be helpful, especially if some simple support strategies are put in place.

It is often helpful for these children if they:

- Practise the letter pattern combinations large scale on a vertical surface so that up and down have meaning.
- Large scale practice also ensures maximum kinaesthetic feedback from the whole hand and arm and from the body moving left to right, rather than feedback from the small movements of the fingers only. This strategy helps to reduce reversals.
- Guidelines should be drawn several inches apart at this stage, with dotted lines for ascenders and descenders.
- The white/black board or paper attached to a wall can be used. An old wallpaper roll can be used effectively at home.
- The use of guidelines may be very useful for all children. The width of the lines should be matched to the average letter size of the child. Every class can benefit from having photocopied guidelines of several widths to match the range of handwriting skills of the children. Narrower lines can gradually be introduced as the writing skills mature.

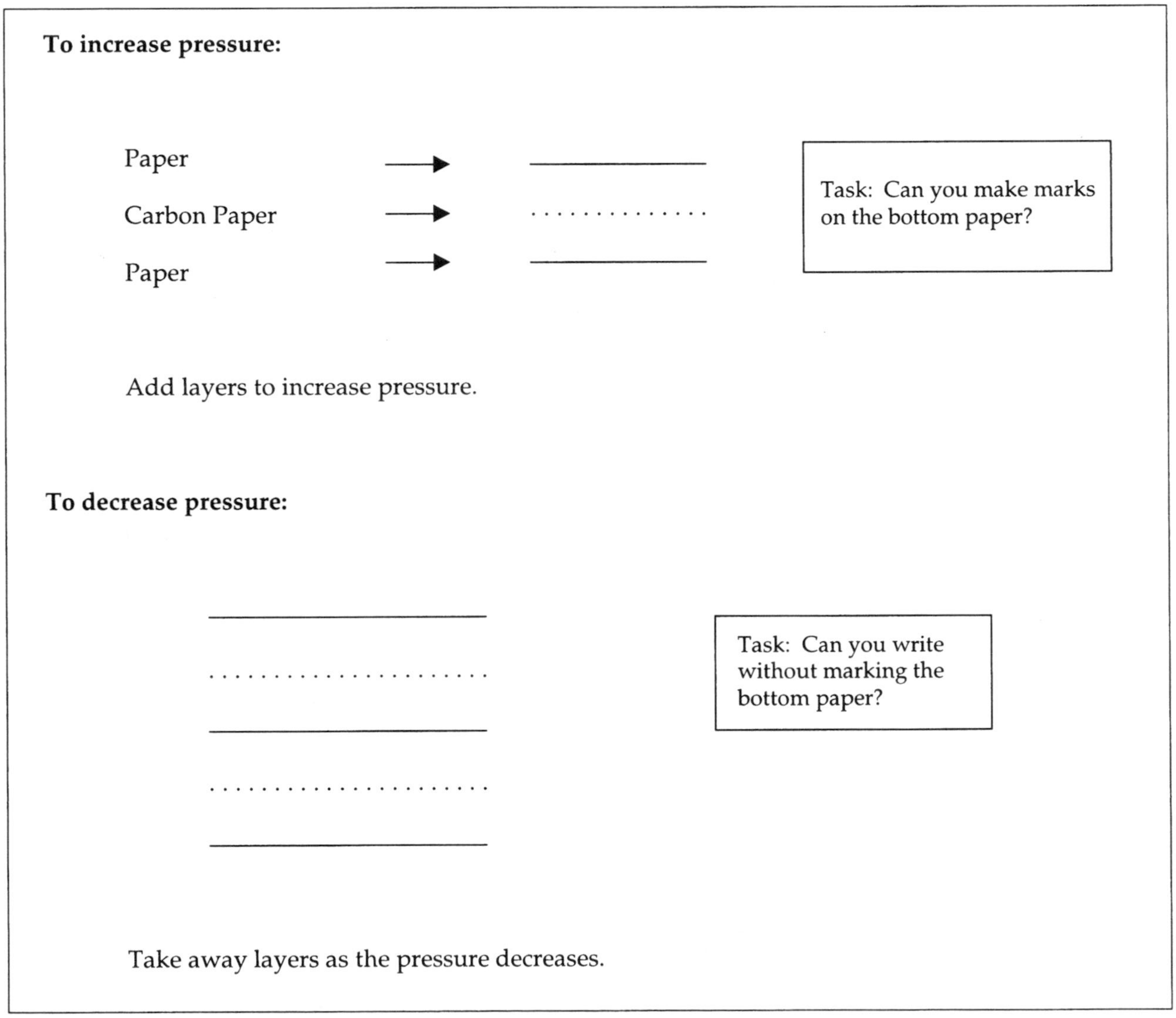

To increase pressure:

Paper	→	————
Carbon Paper	→	· · · · · · · · · · · ·
Paper	→	————

Task: Can you make marks on the bottom paper?

Add layers to increase pressure.

To decrease pressure:

———————

· · · · · · · · · · · · · · · · · · · ·

———————

· · · · · · · · · · · · · · · · · · · ·

———————

Task: Can you write without marking the bottom paper?

Take away layers as the pressure decreases.

Figure 5.1 The carbon paper sandwich

Alternatives to handwriting

For many children who experience difficulties with fine-motor skills, handwriting will be slow to reach the final developmental stage of automaticity. They will still be using mental energy and effort to deal with the mechanics of handwriting while their peers have achieved a degree of automaticity which frees them to attend to style, content, proof-reading, spelling, etc. As discussed in the section on the development of Praxis, in children there is a gradual development of the control of all movement so that it comes under more automatic control. The same sequence applies to walking and picking up objects as to handwriting. It is interesting to note that the opposite trend appears to occur in older people. German studies have shown that adults over 60 perform less well on a memory task if they are required simultaneously to negotiate a simple obstacle course. By contrast, teenagers and mature adults do not perform less well under these conditions. The researchers concluded that as people get older, the automatic control of movement patterns begins to break down so that more mental effort is required for movement control and it again becomes harder to perform other tasks at the same time.

Some children will always struggle with the mechanics of handwriting, and this will affect their ability to demonstrate knowledge and skills unless alternative means of recording can be devised which will enable the student to concentrate on the content of their written work and achieve some degree of independence when recording. Alternatives to handwriting could include:

- The teacher or classroom assistant acting as a scribe.
- The child using a tape recorder or dictaphone and parents or school staff typing or writing what they want to say.
- For older children access to a word processor may be very important, but younger children may not be ready to use a keyboard without supervision.
- The words which the child is able to recognise are written on cards, filed as in a 'Breakthrough to Literacy' folder; the child composes sentences by placing the words in order on a rack or a long card by using Blu-Tack or Velcro. The teacher, classroom assistant or parent helper can make a written record of the child's work.
- Use of diagrams, charts, graphs, mind maps and other forms of visual representation.
- Use of a cartoon grid to record a story or activity and the child draws in or places the pictures in the right order.
- Picture cards that form a sequence with their corresponding sentences; match-order-record.
- Use of appropriate software such as Clicker 4 Software.

Setting out work

Some children with dyspraxia may have difficulties with any form of spatial representation. This may involve three-dimensional space and affect their movements around the environment (see section 'The school environment', p. 47) and also two-dimensional representations. The interpretation of two-dimensional information such as 'reading' maps, graphs and diagrams may be affected, as well as the ability to set out work on paper and to use the available space in the usual way.

In order to help children in setting out their work, the following might be tried:

- Coloured dots: green for starting place, red for the finish and an orange dot to signal don't start a new word after this sign.
- The use of guidelines for writing.
- A template for the setting out of tasks prepared in advance showing, for example, lines for where the heading and date go, a box in which to draw apparatus or a picture, guidelines for writing, (Figure 5.2).

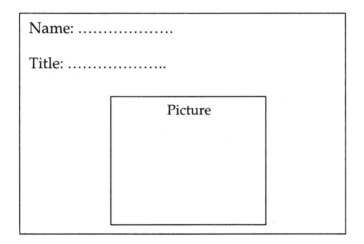

Figure 5.2 Guidelines for writing

- The setting out of a maths task may be particularly difficult and column drift can make it harder to carry out the mathematical processes accurately. Squared paper where the squares are a suitable size for the child's writing size can help, but some children may benefit from a template for each sum, numbered on the page, (Figure 5.3).

Templates can be prepared in advance and the sign for the process (+, -, x, ÷) can be inserted individually if there are 'mixed' examples.

1.		T	U		2.		T	U
+					+			

Figure 5.3 Templates for sums

Reading

Most dyspraxic children will learn to read as well as their peers, unless they have specific phonological problems. However, a few may struggle to learn to read because of difficulties with eye movement control or visual perception.

Ocular-motor dyspraxia

The definition of ocular-motor dyspraxia is the inability to move the eyes independently of head movement, and difficulties with fine-motor control may affect eye movement control in some cases. The visual screening carried out at school or tests of acuity at the optician's may not assess dynamic ocular movements. If a child has difficulties with ocular-motor control, parents or teachers may become aware of difficulties with tasks such as reading, writing or copying from the board. Visual tracking and the localisation of stimuli may be difficult and result in excessive head or even upper body movement as an accompaniment to eye movement.

Below is a quick, easy screening for tracking problems:

- Ask the child to hold their head still with their hand.
- Ask him/her to follow a pencil with their eyes as you move it L-R across the field of vision.
- Look for uncontrolled movements, particularly as you cross the mid-line.

Some of the behavioural signs associated with eye movement control problems while reading are presented in Chapter 2. If a child is showing a significant number (over half) of the signs, on a regular basis, then it is important for the teacher to consider how the process of reading could be made easier for that child. A referral to an optometrist would be appropriate, and eye exercises can give very positive results as shown in Case Study 2.

Environmental changes may also help to support the child, for example:

- use of a piece of card to aid locating text on the page;
- access to enlarged text – enlarged photocopies may be helpful;
- access to a bar magnifier;
- reading from a text held vertically;
- shared reading, using appropriate font size, to practise the eye movements, following a moving finger;
- reading from a computer screen with a cursor moving left to right across the screen following the text;
- projecting the text onto a distant vertical surface to minimise the effort needed for convergence;
- keeping worksheets simple by reducing the number of items on each page, thus reducing visual search;
- practice in visual scanning and visual search, using picture material.

Visual perception

Some children will have difficulties with aspects of spatial perception which may first become apparent as they attempt to move around the classroom without bumping into objects or other people. Avoiding moving objects and people on the playground or during PE may be even more difficult.

In some cases, the difficulties with spatial perception may affect the ability to interpret visual-spatial information such as pictures, diagrams, graphs or maps. Modifications of the material to give more visual clarity may help, but strategies may have to be individualised for each child.

Copying

Many of the routine tasks undertaken by children in class require copying, either from a board or a worksheet; copying from a book, worksheet or a board combines the skills of eye movement control with those needed for handwriting. For children who have difficulties in either area it is best to try to avoid copying tasks whenever possible, because they involve:

- locating the place on the board, book or worksheet;
- retaining the information;
- locating the place where the information is to be recorded;
- recording.

Of the four phases, only the retention of information may be unaffected by fine-motor difficulties. Teachers need to be aware that the effort required to complete the task might be out of all proportion to the academic benefits of completing the task, and so such tasks should be kept to a minimum. If there is no alternative, copying from a prepared sheet on the desk/table will be easier than attempting to copy a distant text. The prepared sheet can be visually simplified by using a larger font and double spacing.

Organisational skills

The organisation of equipment

Some children find it hard to organise the equipment that they need in order to carry out a task.

For small children

- The first step may be to have their essential equipment for the task ready in a box or tray so that they can get started on the task.
- At suitable times during the school day play the 'fetch me game' using verbal and/or picture prompts, until the child is able to find all the commonly used classroom equipment.
- Once all items can be found, start to leave a picture of the missing item from the tray on the desk so that one item has to be fetched. Backward chaining is used until the child is able to fetch all the equipment using the picture cues as prompts.
- Gradually fade out the picture cues.

For older children

- The teacher might have a pack of cue cards showing items of equipment which are needed for the task. As s/he is explaining what will be needed, the relevant cards are dealt onto a Velcro strip attached to the child's table (see Figure 5.4).
- As a whole-class approach, the cue cards can be larger and attached to a strip which is available for all to see. Many children in a class will benefit from this approach.
- Written language can be used once the children have a relevant sight vocabulary. The transition can be managed by having the pictures and words displayed together at first.

Prompt sheets for familiar tasks can be prepared in advance (Figure 5.5).

Organisation of tasks

Some children who have sequencing problems may find it hard to carry out a task which has more than one step. Picture or written flow charts can be helpful. For example, Figure 5.6 is a flow chart for the task of colouring a picture of a bird and sticking it on the collage.

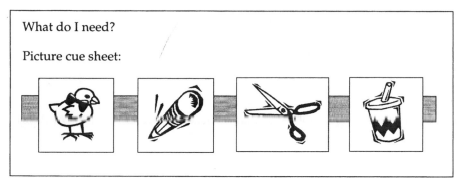

Figure 5.4 A cue sheet for the organisation of equipment

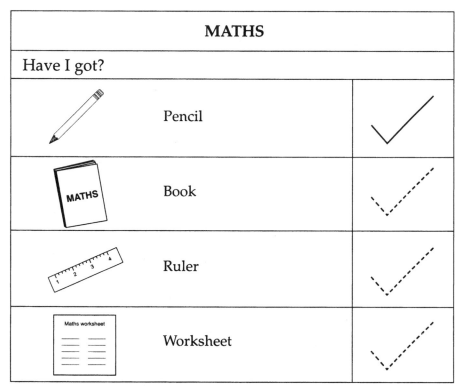

Figure 5.5 A cue sheet for the organisation of equipment

Flow charts for maths problems may be particularly useful, as shown in Figure 5.7.

For instructions involving more than one element, teachers can photocopy flow charts with 2→ (n) boxes and the teacher or LSA might draw or write the stages of complex instructions in the relevant boxes.

1. The school environment

Other possible challenges in Key Stages 1 and 2

- Children may have difficulties 'navigating' around the school. Colour coding of doors and coloured footprints or guidelines can be helpful and reassuring to many young children as well as to the dyspraxic child.
- Children may have difficulty navigating around the classroom without bumping into tables and other children, stumbling over

objects and knocking things over. Seating where they have a clear run to the equipment they are likely to need and out of busy areas may prevent disruption to peers and embarrassment for the child.

- Acknowledge that every school does have children for whom conventional playtime is stressful.
- Provide an alternative option to going out for active physical play, such as a games activity room where there are table-top games, construction toys, etc.
- Provide the option of an adult-led game in the playground in which vulnerable children can be included.

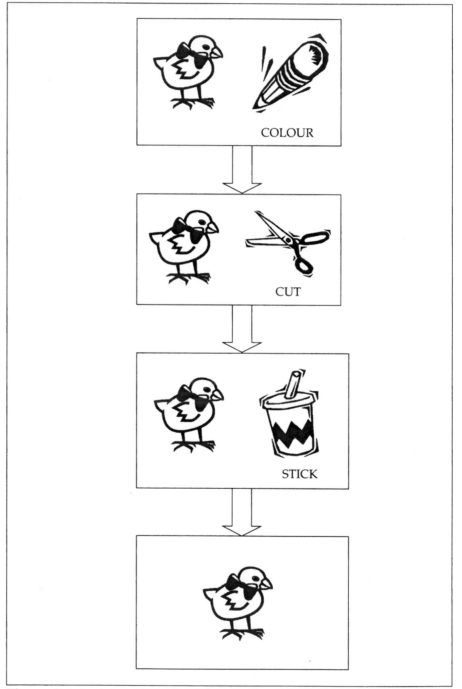

Figure 5.6 A picture cue sheet for a task

- Landscape the play areas so that there are quiet areas for sitting, talking or less active forms of play.
- Provide useful jobs for vulnerable children to do in small groups, indoors or outside, so that they are less obvious targets than they would be as a lone child who does not appear to be doing anything.
- Establish social skills groups and circle of friends.

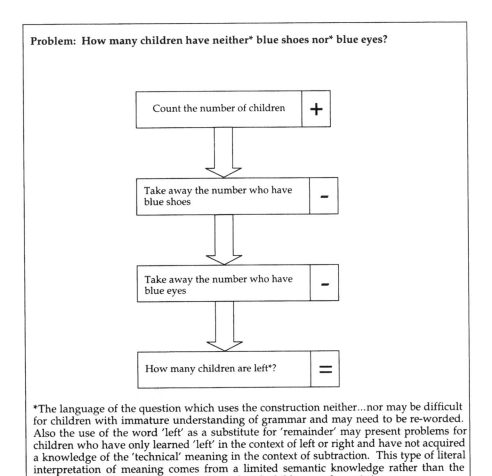

Problem: How many children have neither* blue shoes nor* blue eyes?

*The language of the question which uses the construction neither...nor may be difficult for children with immature understanding of grammar and may need to be re-worded. Also the use of the word 'left' as a substitute for 'remainder' may present problems for children who have only learned 'left' in the context of left or right and have not acquired a knowledge of the 'technical' meaning in the context of subtraction. This type of literal interpretation of meaning comes from a limited semantic knowledge rather than the literal interpretations which are associated with children on the autistic spectrum.

Figure 5.7 A flow chart for a maths problem

2. Dressing and undressing

This activity is often associated with PE/games which may be stressful in their own right. Many children will have difficulty with buttons, shoelaces, buckles and other clothing items when they start school, so Early Years teachers and classroom assistants are familiar with both helping children and encouraging them to do things independently.

Children with dyspraxia/DCD may have significant problems with dressing, and it may be assumed that a child has had these things done for them at home and therefore the skills have not developed. However, for children who have dyspraxia, learning to achieve the skills independently will be hard and they might never get to school on time if left to their own devices.

Typically children may have problems with:

- fastenings;
- putting clothing on, e.g. socks onto the foot; trousers with a leg in each trouser leg, T-shirts over the head;
- knowing the order they need to put clothing on, e.g. pants before trousers;
- knowing which items of clothing match to which areas of the body.

It may be necessary to work with the occupational therapist and the child's parents to follow an individually designed dressing programme.

Some of the activities discussed in Chapter 8 do help to promote the body awareness necessary for efficient dressing, e.g. putting quoits over feet and hands in a rhythmic sequence, as in Figure 5.7. The child sits supported, with back against a wall or on a chair and puts a quoit on each foot in turn; then a quoit on each hand in turn.

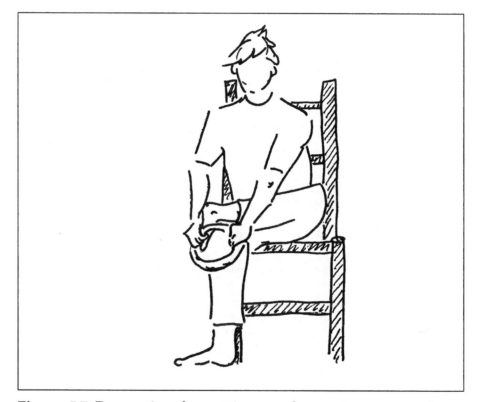

Figure 5.7 Preparation for putting on sleeves, trousers, socks or gloves

Similarly, Figure 5.8 shows an exercise in which the child passes a hoop over the body and then steps out of it. The hoop is passed over the head as a prelude to putting on T-shirts, jumpers, etc. The hoop is passed up the body as a prelude to putting on trousers etc.

Some specific strategies such as backward chaining may be used, as shown in Figure 5.9.

It is best to have the children seated for these activities, especially if they have poor balance and postural control.

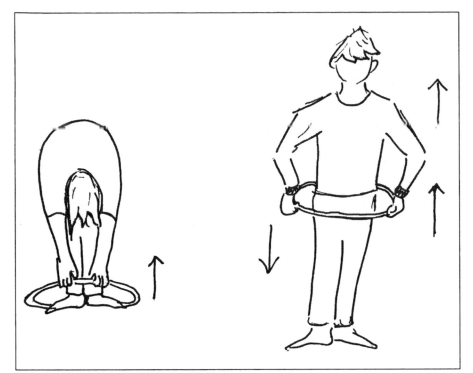

Figure 5.8 A hoop exercise as preparation for dressing

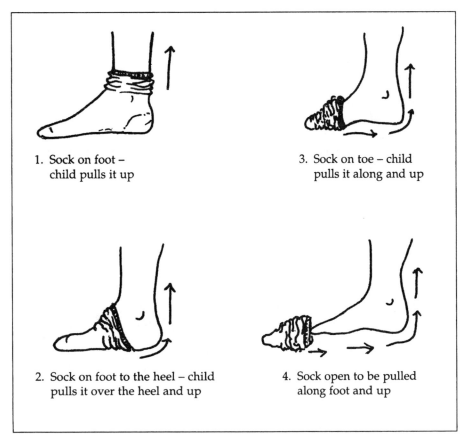

1. Sock on foot – child pulls it up

3. Sock on toe – child pulls it along and up

2. Sock on foot to the heel – child pulls it over the heel and up

4. Sock open to be pulled along foot and up

Figure 5.9 Backward chaining

Other quick tips

- The marking of items of clothing may help, e.g. a red dot on the right shoe, trouser leg, arm of the jumper.
- Give reminders that logos go at the front of tops and labels at the back.
- Select shoes with Velcro rather than buckles or laces, and T-shirts and jumpers rather than shirts which have buttons.
- Use elasticated neckties.
- Recommend spiral shoelaces and other devices, so that laces do not need to be tied.

Dressing and undressing are often done under time pressure at school (changing for PE) and at home (getting ready for school). It is helpful to teach and practise the skills when there is no time pressure, as part of the IEP which is supported at home and planned jointly with the occupational therapist. It is helpful to remember that dyspraxic children are classic cases of 'less haste more speed' so that exhortations to hurry may disrupt the motor skills which are emerging.

3. Balance and posture

Some children, particularly in the Early Years, experience difficulties with the maintenance of balance and posture. Parents often report that their child falls over frequently and bumps into people and the furniture.

Children who find it hard to maintain balance may have difficulty standing still, e.g. when lining up, and may appear to fidget and lean on the wall, furniture or other children.

They may also find it hard to maintain the balance of their upper body without leaning on the table, their arms or other nearby things. They may constantly be readjusting their position and find it hard to free up their arms and hands to perform table-top activities. These children have their best chance of maintaining balance when they are seated on a chair which has back and possibly arm support and they can put both feet flat on the floor. They may have to be helped to establish, and reminded to maintain, their posture. They are likely to be most noticeable when they are required to sit on the carpet. The lack of support combined with poor balance and trunk stability may make this an almost impossible task. They may be observed continually adjusting their position, often falling onto or 'kicking' other children, or giving up and lying on the floor. This behaviour is inevitably seen as disruptive by staff and peers. It is also very difficult to give attention to listening and thinking when much of your attention is devoted to trying to maintain your body in an upright position.

Other children who have a weak proprioceptive system may continually appear to be making minor movements, fiddling with objects in the vicinity or touching parts of their own body. These movements are largely unconscious and serve to stimulate the proprioceptive system to give feedback about where parts of their body are in space and what they are in contact with – bottom on the seat, fingers on the desk, etc.

CASE STUDY 8

A, Year 2

A only just escaped being prescribed Ritalin. He found it hard to stay on his seat when he attempted table-top activities so he was on and off the chair, sometimes kneeling on the floor, sometimes standing up. At carpet times he rolled on the floor, 'kicked' other children, leant on other children, fell over the others' legs when making his way to his place near the teacher, and never appeared to take in what the teacher was saying.

- A was supplied with furniture which allowed him to sit on the chair with feet on the ground.
- His table was against a wall so he could lean with his shoulder on the wall for support. A chair with arms might have been a preferred option.
- A was given short tasks with legitimate opportunities to move from his table between his tasks.
- The seating arrangements for 'carpet time' were changed for the class so there were always options to sit on chairs round the circle or use the beanbags. A was subtly directed to one of these alternatives each time.

He started to listen and participate in the activities so the 'disruptive' behaviour was no longer a problem.

4. PE and games

Children who have poor motor skills have often had less experience of exploring their environment and testing out their motor competence. They may present as unduly timid, e.g. unwilling to attempt a small jump off a bench, or without a sense of danger, e.g. launching themselves off apparatus with little apparent regard for safety.

The teaching and practice of gross-motor skills as described in the final chapter should be an important part of their learning experience which will promote their self-esteem and social inclusion.

Preparation for transition

For some children with dyspraxia/DCD many of the key issues at Key Stages 1 and 2 may be resolved by the time they transfer to the secondary phase of their education. Other issues, particularly those around handwriting, setting out work and self-organisation, are likely to persist while the educational environment presents new challenges for them to meet.

Case Study 9 presents a pen-portrait of a boy at the start of Year 6, and illustrates some of the complexities which may be associated with dyspraxia at this stage.

CASE STUDY 9

T, Year 6

T has a good general knowledge and vocabulary. At ten, his favourite TV programme is *Horizon*, and he understands and remembers what he heard or saw. Assessments carried out by the educational psychologist showed that his abilities were well above average. However, his early articulatory dyspraxia and phonological problems affect the intelligibility of his speech when he is excited, tired or anxious, and contribute to his difficulties with reading and spelling. Although an optician would say that his vision is normal, he has difficulties with the control of his eye movements – convergence, pursuit and tracking – which also make reading and copying difficult for T. He never reads for long periods.

T is able, at last, to write neatly, albeit slowly, but he can only sustain his effort for short periods of time. His short bursts of concentrated effort and his fatigue towards the end of the day or the week contribute to a variability in his performance that is hard for some of his teachers to accept.

T has difficulties with body control and balance so he appears to be restless and to fidget in his seat and not to stand still in line. He often trips over things and bumps into people as he moves around the classroom, but most of his classmates have known him for years and are quite tolerant. T's mother is aware that he can get lost even in his familiar junior school and wonders how he will cope with moving around a big secondary school.

T's body awareness is poor but he can now dress himself without help, provided no one rushes him. He finds it hard to organise his possessions, his tasks and his equipment, and so his teacher has been advised to use visual cue cards to help him with this. Year 5 had been quite difficult for T because some of the topics in maths, technology and science involved him using equipment in a coordinated way and T finds it hard to coordinate even tasks such as using a ruler to draw a line.

Perhaps because he is such an able boy, T finds it hard to accept how difficult it is for him to do some things which his classmates find easy. He has really good ideas but is unable to write them down and often goes for the easy option of writing something short and predictable which only uses the simple words that he is able to spell. His teacher tries to give him opportunities to show his skills in class discussions and mental arithmetic sessions. Unfortunately, T's ideal-self is to be good at all the things his peers can do and he values activities such as reading, writing, completing classroom assignments and playing football. He tends to dismiss his areas of strength as unimportant and so his self-esteem remains low.

Chapter 6

Key Issues for Key Stages 3 and 4

Secondary transfer presents all children with new challenges and opportunities. Children with special needs, including dyspraxia/DCD, are no exception to this, but a successful transition does have to be carefully planned and managed. This chapter attempts to highlight the aspects of secondary school that may have disproportionately more impact on a child with dyspraxia/DCD.

In many cases, the planning for transition will begin in Year 6 at least two terms before the child is due to change school. For students who have a statement of special educational needs, the annual review prior to transfer would usually take place in the autumn term and involve the SENCO and/or Year 7 coordinator for the secondary school.

Four steps have been identified for promoting successful transition:

Transition into secondary school

Step 1: A meeting of the key people

This should include:

- key school staff (form tutor, SENCO and year head);
- key school staff from previous school;
- professionals concerned (e.g. educational psychologist, social worker);
- parents;
- the student themselves, if able to cope.

The annual review, if the child has a statement of special educational needs, might be an appropriate forum for this meeting.
The meeting should:

- identify the pupil's strengths and areas of difficulty;
- share information on successful and unsuccessful strategies used to date;
- anticipate and plan for the changes and expectations inherent in the new situation;
- identify a plan for introducing the pupil to the new school environment;
- identify key person(s) responsible for liaison over the initial 'settling in' period.

Step 2: A staff development session to raise awareness

This should be organised prior to the pupil's arrival and should include all staff who are likely to come across the child, including dinner supervisors, playground assistants, caretaker, etc.

It is also a good idea to invite the pupil's parents to the meeting and to ask them to contribute if they feel able to do so. Alternatively, show a video of the child introducing him/herself and showing aspects of classroom and playground experiences at primary school.

The staff session should cover:

- a discussion about Praxis and how it develops;
- the features associated with dyspraxia that this student shows;
- how best to help the young person;
- how to help other pupils help the young person with dyspraxia;
- where to obtain literature, references, video material, etc.;
- who is the key member of staff to seek out if there are problems.

It is recommended that the school asks a professional with expertise in the area to give input to this staff development session unless there is specialist knowledge and experience within the staff group. An approach to the educational psychology service, teaching support services or to the school adviser/advisory teacher should enable a school to be put in touch with someone who can help.

Step 3: A plan of what to say to other pupils

Many students with dyspraxia are able to take their place among their peers without any significant social difficulties, although making and keeping friends may become an issue which needs to be addressed.

However, situations may arise in PE, practical lessons and even when written work is required, which draw attention to the coordination problems which the student experiences. Other students sometimes resent any special concessions or different treatment of a fellow student unless they understand why that person is unlucky enough not to be able to do certain things as well as they can.

- Where it seems appropriate, talk to the other pupils about the difficulties the pupil with dyspraxia might face. This needs to be done with sensitivity and in consultation with parents, but if done well, it can protect the young person from the effects of ignorance, misunderstanding and resentment.
- For older pupils, the following kind of explanation can be helpful: *'You know what dyslexia is? A difficulty reading words. Well, Jamie has a difficulty with his balance and coordination he finds ... hard.'*
- Emphasise the strengths and skills of the pupil with dyspraxia and how they can be useful socially (e.g. Jamie may not be much good at cricket but he may be excellent at keeping score).
- Elicit the help of older pupils in watching out for the pupil with dyspraxia at playtimes and acknowledging them in a friendly way. Friendly acknowledgement can often be immensely important and reassuring.

- An older 'buddy' who has experienced similar difficulties may be an important ally and mentor for a new student.

Step 4: Introducing the pupil to the school

The large campus, frequent room changes, the need to organise books, equipment and time as well as the curriculum demands, are likely to be confusing and anxiety provoking for a student with dyspraxia. The following are recommended as strategies:

- Establish a rapport and an open channel of communication with the young person's parents.
- Elicit from the parents and the young person themselves the anxieties, likely trouble spots and the successful strategies used at home.
- Where possible, the pupil with dyspraxia should visit their new school out of school hours and have a chance to familiarise themselves with layout and the geography of classroom, assembly hall, toilets, dinner hall, cloakroom, etc.
- Arrange additional familiarisation visits on which to practise moving around the campus and finding specific teaching bases from the tutor room. This will help the student build a mental map of the layout of the building before attempting to move between lessons in crowded corridors.
- Give the student a map of the school campus with the rooms they will use clearly marked.
- Give the young person a 'timetable' with the rooms marked. Go through it with them carefully because the more able a pupil feels to predict the routine of the school, the more confident they will feel. Let the young person keep the timetable for reference.
- Give the pupil a written or pictorial representation of the key school rules. Go over them and let them take a copy away for reference.
- Explain carefully any equipment needs and discuss with parents the suggestions in the section on 'organisation of equipment', (e.g. bag, pencil, ruler, etc.).
- Introduce the pupil to key staff and identify to them the key staff member to approach if there is a problem. Discuss where they can be found and when (e.g. at breaktime, not during maths!) and what to do if a problem occurs outside these times, or if the key staff member is unavailable.
- For the pupil with reading skills, write everything down and make sure the pupil has it for reference.

Recording information

The majority of students entering Year 7 will have reached the final phase in the development of their handwriting skills. The writing of high-frequency familiar words will no longer require visual monitoring; letter size, formation and spacing will all be fluent and demand, in themselves, a minimal focus of attention. Handwriting will have become an efficient tool for recording information, and the speed of recording will increase gradually from an average of 18 words per minute at 12 years to 23 wpm at 18 years. (Handwriting norms are presented in Appendix III.)

Students who have not achieved automaticity by the start of the secondary phase of their education will be ill placed to meet the output demands of the secondary curriculum. Handwriting will remain slow and take up a disproportionate amount of attention and effort, so that:

- Reduced stamina will affect the quantity of output, particularly when there are time limits to complete a task.
- Taking notes and copying from a text or board will be too slow to keep pace with the rest of the group.
- Written assignments may be limited to the minimum in terms of quantity and quality, affecting sentence structure, range of vocabulary and development of ideas.

For students who experience significant difficulties with handwriting, alternative means of recording will need to be considered:

Alternatives to taking notes

- LSA takes notes for the students who have dyspraxia, dyslexia and other special needs.
- Pre-prepared notes are distributed to students, who use a highlighter pen to keyword the text.
- Tape-recording.

Support for taking notes

- Student is trained in icon note-taking techniques, (see Figure 6.1). No one else needs to understand the message, only the person who makes the notes.

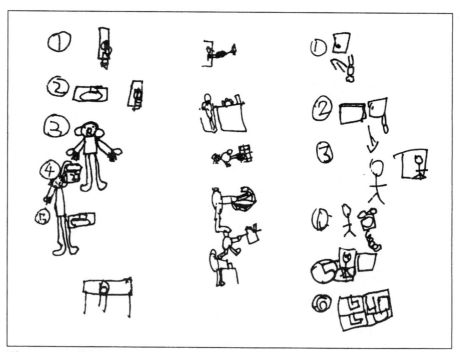

Figure 6.1 KS 2 examples of icon note-taking

- Student develops a personal shorthand for high-frequency and topic-related vocabulary, e.g.

  The = ^   Because = ∴.   Individual = |°

- Student trained to use mind-mapping techniques, unless problems with spatial representations are a component of the dyspraxia.
- When students do need to hand write, an A4 file can make a discreet sloping surface and extra time should be allowed.
- Copying tasks should be avoided if possible. A text might be photocopied and the student use a highlighter to keyword the text.

Recording homework accurately may be difficult and most schools have systems for recording homework for students who do have problems with this.

Students may be willing to accept a scribe in lessons which require a significant amount of writing and for SATs. Some students are embarrassed by this and alternative strategies will be needed.

Information technology as an alternative to handwriting

- A robust, portable laptop may be recommended for a student who has severe difficulties.
- Access to word processing facilities and a printer may be arranged in the SEN/ICT departments for students with less severe difficulties.
- Students may benefit from a touch-typing tutor course which they access in the SEN department to speed up their keyboard skills. Some students do resist learning to touch-type and prefer to stay with a two-fingered approach.
- ICT assessors may say that a dyspraxic student is not 'suitable' for the allocation of a laptop. It needs to be emphasised that it may take longer for the student to develop the skills but the pay-off in terms of legibility and presentation will be very significant.
- The aim for the student, however they choose to use the keyboard, should be that their typing is at least as quick as handwriting by the time they start the GCSE courses in Year 10.
- Students who have difficulties with spatial planning will benefit from a graphics package to support the production of graphs, diagrams, technical drawings, apparatus. The Pictures for Projects Program is useful for secondary-aged students.

Presentation and setting out work

The same strategies that are used in Key Stage 2 may be discreetly used at Key Stages 3 and 4 if required. Use of information technology begins to take over from these once the student becomes proficient.

Students who experience difficulties with the mechanics of handwriting also, frequently, have difficulties with spelling. Learning spellings from computer programs which present a clear consistent visual image of the word can help. Their own inconsistent attempts at writing make strategies such as look/cover/write much less effective for these students.

CASE STUDY 10 (part 1)

F, Year 8

In Year 5, F had been identified as dyspraxic with particular difficulties in the areas of:

- sensory processing;
- balance;
- speed and smoothness of movements, particularly fine movements which affected his handwriting to a significant degree.

In Year 8 he was re-referred to the educational psychology service because of concerns that his ability to record information did not reflect the verbal abilities that he was able to demonstrate in class. (He obtained a score at 86th percentile for verbal abilities.)

F said that he had been teased in Year 7 and less so in Year 8. Incidents had been noted in Year 7 and dealt with in school.

F was aware that his organisation and coordination problems affected the speed of his handwriting and his participation in practical sessions for science and technology.

Assessment indicated:

- Handwriting speed was 10 wpm regardless of whether he was asked to write at his own pace or as quickly as possible. It is quite common for students with dyspraxia that an instruction to write quickly results in reduced legibility but no real increase in speed and performance.
- Standardised assessments (WISC R Coding and Beery Test of Visual-Motor Integration) indicated an age-equivalent skill level for pencil and paper tasks of between 6 and 6½ years. F was, therefore, attempting to access a secondary curriculum with motor skills for handwriting which are more typical of a Year 2 or 3 child.

The problems that F reported are consistent with the results of the assessment:

- keeping up when note-taking;
- copying from a board or a book;
- taking down information, including homework, in time;
- completing written tasks in the time available;
- spending excessive time on written homework;
- writing for any length of time because of tensions in his hand.

The problems that F reported with practical tasks were consistent with his attempts to carry out a block design task, so that he had problems with:

- left-right orientation;
- manipulation of the materials;
- speed of task completion – so that he obtained few bonus marks.

F did manage to complete the designs, which suggested that he had a clear idea in his head about the patterns he wanted to produce. He was clearly frustrated by his limited ability to execute his motor plan, but did not appear to have significant difficulties with the spatial planning aspect of the task.

Visual perception and ocular-motor control

Some students with dyspraxia will experience difficulties with visual perception which affect their ability to interpret and to reproduce information which is presented spatially. This might involve three-dimensional representations such as assembling apparatus for chemistry or molecular models in physics. It might also involve the two-dimensional spatial representations which occur across the whole range of the curriculum – graphs, diagrams, maps, charts and, in some cases, even picture material. Those students can be supported if these spatial images are:

- simplified and have the most significant elements highlighted in some way;
- enlarged or the number of them on a page reduced.

In addition:

- Mechanical supports such as rulers or mechanical strips to help with the 'reading' of graphs or map references may be provided.
- The drawing of maps and diagrams may be difficult so it is often appropriate to give an outline to the student who then labels the appropriate features. For students with extreme handwriting problems, the placing of pre-printed labels may be required.

Some students may have a legacy of poor literacy skills which can be linked to difficulties with visual-perception and/or ocular-motor dyspraxia. Their needs are then very similar to those of other students who experience specific learning difficulties/dyslexia, and the same support systems are appropriate.

However, students who have problems with ocular-motor control may have additional difficulties with:

- scanning for information from a text or dictionary;
- finding and maintaining their place in a text;
- copying – especially from a board;
- sustaining reading over time, especially in the evenings when they are tired;
- reading small print, especially if there are many lines on the page;
- reading text which is printed over a diagram or picture.

CASE STUDY 10 (part 2)

F, Year 8

F had first been identified in Year 4 as a boy with reading difficulties and his dyspraxic diagnosis came later. He had been given eye exercises in the past but he admitted that he had not followed them with any consistency. A quick screening test indicated that he still had problems with convergence at the standard reading distance. His reading had improved over the years, 16th percentile by Year 8, but he did not read for pleasure, and decoding remained a slow, laborious process for him. He had particular difficulties with dense, small-sized print and so some texts and worksheets were simplified or enlarged for him.

Organisational skills

1. Organisation of tasks and equipment

- Students with dyspraxia/DCD do experience great difficulties with the organisation of their books and equipment. It is often helpful if in Year 7, parents and a named person in school are able to check that these students have the books and equipment needed for the morning, for the afternoon and for completing their homework. The final session also provides a useful opportunity to ensure that they have the homework written down and know what to do. Responsibility for books and equipment can gradually be taken over by the student, with checklists as a helpful prompt.
- A bag with small accessible pockets for key items of equipment which are needed frequently, e.g. planner, pen and pencil, calculator, is helpful. This avoids having to search for these in the main compartment of the school bag.
- Students with proprioceptive problems often have difficulties identifying objects by touch in a bag and so there is always the danger that they will end up tipping out everything in their bag at the start of a lesson. They then spend time collecting up the debris and miss vital information at the start of a lesson.

The use of transparent zip wallets with a different colour fastener for each subject can help to avoid this problem. All the equipment, books and worksheets, needed for a subject such as maths may be in the red wallet. They only need to get out that wallet and repack it at the end of the lesson. A transparent pencil case is also a sensible choice.

2. Navigation around the school

- If a dyspraxic student has a heavy bag and specialist equipment to carry around the school campus there may be issues of stamina to consider. It is sometimes possible for the student to have access to a locker so they do not have to carry everything around with them all day. A buddy system can sometimes be set up so that friends are enlisted to help with the carrying of equipment.
- For students who have problems with balance, going up and down stairs at busy times of the day may be hazardous, and arrangements may need to be made so that they can leave lessons a little early.
- Learning to navigate around the school may be initially problematic and this is discussed in the section on transition.

3. The organisation of tasks and processes

- The strategies which are suggested to help children in Key Stage 2 to gather their equipment, work through tasks which involve a sequence of activities, and clarify the steps in a problem-solving process, are all equally appropriate in Key Stage 3, provided the presentation style is more adult in appearance.
- Students may experience particular problems when longer assignments are set which cover several homeworks or an extended time period. They may need help to break the task into manageable sub-goals with a specific date for the achievement of

that target. Most students need help to do this when they first face this challenge, and dyspraxic students will need to have the structure supported for longer.

- The aim should be for them to develop the skills which enable them to take responsibility for the planning themselves.

4. Homework

Homework can be a particular source of stress to the child, to parents and to teaching staff. Some special arrangements may have to be considered:

- the differentiation of homework tasks, e.g. to minimise the written component;
- a clear message that alternatives to handwriting such as the use of a word processor, a scribe or a tape are acceptable;
- time to use the word processor and printer in school if these are not available at home;
- request to subject teachers or classroom assistants to write homework in the homework diary;
- time in support studies to help with homework assignments that the student has found difficult;
- support in advance to organise topic work or projects which will extend over several homeworks;
- a clear message that the homework should only take 'x' minutes and that it is acceptable not to finish if parents sign the work to say that the student did try for that amount of time;
- a homework club after school when any students can receive support for assignments that they may find difficult.

Some students find it very difficult to follow homework routines when the lesson might be on Monday, homework to be done Tuesday, homework to be handed in on Thursday. The use of stacker boxes at home can help with this organisational nightmare, (see Figure 6.2).

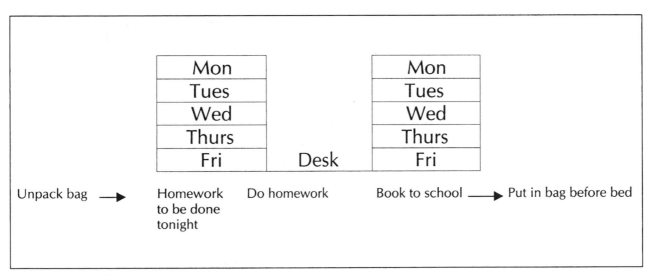

Figure 6.2 Stacker boxes for organising homework

Students may need help to organise the system at first and a few boys have not accepted it enough to take over responsibility for themselves. However, at least one of these students has been known spontaneously to have re-established the system when he went to college.

5. The organisation of time

Students who have dyspraxia are often not good at changing the rate of their writing, dressing or other aspects of motor performance in order to adapt to time restraints. They may also have poor time concepts as younger children and be poor at estimating how long an activity might take.

This was a particular issue for the boy cited in Case Study 10. His mother was very concerned that he would never be able to time routines, e.g. getting ready to catch the bus to college, without support. It was decided that he would use a kitchen timer to estimate how long specific tasks, e.g. showering, dressing, would take, set the timer and then record how accurate his estimation had been. The work progressed so that he has become more aware of time and time constraints and has started to work back from deadlines and decide when he needs to start something in order to finish on time.

6. Subject-specific difficulties

- The manipulation of equipment may be difficult for students with dyspraxia. This may extend to drawing a line with a ruler or using a compass as well as handling delicate equipment:

> V wanted to do physics at GCSE and a skill-based assessment indicated that provided that he had extra time in practical sessions and access to alternative means for recording, including 'Pictures for Projects' software, he could manage all but soldering quite independently.

- Practical lessons such as science, technology and food science may present a safety issue:

> H and his father discussed safety and decided that it would be more acceptable for H to watch some experiments rather than to participate actively. H felt more comfortable about this than having an LSA to help him because he thought that would be embarrassing.

- Many subjects do involve working as a member of a group and from primary school days a person who is likely to drop things, knock them over, miss when pouring, not be able to balance the marble, etc. is not likely to be chosen as a partner or group member.

Subject teachers should be aware of a student's difficulties and encourage pairings and groups in a sensitive way. The allocation of specific roles within a group which provide the opportunity for a student to display competence is often helpful. Students with dyspraxia/DCD might not be asked to record data or enter it on the graph but rather read the instructions, report verbally on observations, collect verbal data on tape, etc.

- Fieldwork may be a source of anxiety and difficulty for some dyspraxic students. Stamina for walking, map reading, navigational skills, and ability to record under difficult conditions, may affect their ability to participate effectively. Support may need to be arranged to ensure that they are fully included.

- The PE and games curriculum has traditionally been a major hazard for students with dyspraxia/DCD. Their core difficulties with balance, the coordination of movement sequences, control of the direction, force and amplitude of movement, smoothness and fluency of movement are all potentially under the spotlight. The response may too often be days off school for stomach/head/leg aches and/or 'forgetting' kit.

Fortunately, most PE departments in secondary schools are now much more sensitive to the needs of students who are not gifted in the area of motor skills. Alternatives to team and racket games which offer the students the fitness programmes they need are often available, but there may be arbitrary rules about which terms these are offered or which year group is able to participate. These rules need to be applied flexibly for students with motor-skill problems. Opportunities to improve fitness by the setting of individual skill targets is accepted in leisure facilities and increasingly in schools.

Swimming, where the water supports the body, is a sport in which dyspraxic children can often compete on more equal terms with their peers.

Case Study 11 presents a pen-portrait of a boy who had significant difficulties at primary school but who only shows residual, albeit significant, problems by Year 9.

CASE STUDY 11

B, Year 9

Developmental history

His mother described B as a boy with good social skills but not very assertive. He has friends in school and has an easygoing, confident persona. His memory and verbal skills were described as areas of strength.

His mother also discussed B's developmental history and reported a slow acquisition of motor and self-help skills.

[continued over]

Gross-motor skill problems:

- balance – bike riding achieved at about eight years, kicking a ball late;
- frequent falls;
- dropping things;
- running in space, avoiding people and objects in the environment.

He tended to stay close to her while other children ran off and explored their environment.

Fine-motor skill problems:

- handwriting;
- coordination of eating with cutlery;
- dressing – fastenings and the order of items.

At 14.01 years, B still has problems with:

- navigating in space without bumping into things – a problem also noted for team games;
- fastening ties and laces;
- handwriting;
- learning new motor skills such as the keyboard.

Specific problems at home were:

Problem	Suggestions discussed
• the organisation of his bedroom	labelling
• the organisation of books for homework	a stacker box system
• time awareness	1. estimating how long a task will take using a timer. 2. planning back from a goal, e.g. the time the bus leaves. 3. using wall planners and calendars

School perceptions – comments from subject teachers

Strengths

1. articulate;
2. understanding better than written output would indicate (mentioned twice);
3. able in the group.

Difficulties

1. settling to task;
2. reluctance to do written work, work independently;
3. homework completion (mentioned four times);

4. organisation;
5. lack of detail in written responses;
6. work poorly presented;
7. confidence in handling tools and materials;
8. following instructions in art and textiles (spatial concepts);
9. variable performance/behaviour reported as quiet in some groups, noisy in others;
10. in PE his skills are at an acceptable level but he can appear clumsy and has problems with the spatial aspects of team games.

Assessment

Beery Test of Visual Motor Integration – 11 year age equivalent
Handwriting 13 wpm

B was asked to perform a number of pencil and paper tasks which he was able to achieve at an acceptable level by working slowly and carefully and using strategies to compensate for the lack of fluency and automaticity in his motor skills. These included:

- taking the pencil off the paper and accommodating changes of direction by changing his direction of movement;
- moving his upper body;
- rotating the paper;
- exerting excessive pressure on the paper.

Wechsler Intelligence Scale for Children (WISC)

Block Design: Scaled Score = 8

Able to verbalise how a block should go but struggled to manipulate the materials to fit his motor plan.

Evidence of frustration at his failure to execute the motor plan effectively.

Summary and conclusions

B's early developmental history does indicate that he has a motor difficulty, probably best classified as a Developmental Co-ordination Disorder. He has by Year 9 achieved many of the basic self-help and motor skills which he has struggled with in the past. The remaining areas of difficulty are connected with his handwriting and his consequent reluctance to engage with written tasks.

Suggestions

1. Access to word processing facilities should help with:
   - ease of completing written assignments;
   - presentation of work including the organisation on the page;
   - proof-reading and correcting work.
2. In order to benefit from this he will need to learn to touch-type to a respectable speed. The Typing Tutor tapes are available at school.

3. Access to word processing facilities for homework assignments would be helpful, especially once he starts his GSCE programme in Year 10.
4. Students who use word processing for assignments during course work are able to use the same facilities in GCSE examinations.
5. The use of writing frames for work which he is unable to do using a word processor would help with the layout/organisation on the page.
6. The use of flow charts for the steps in a problem-solving process may help B to organise his tasks.
7. A scribe for SATs – if B would find that acceptable, since his typing speed will need time and practice to reach a useful level.

SENCO to investigate whether he needs help in science and technology as he is reported to have problems with the manipulation of tools and materials in textiles.

Chapter 7

Case Study Examples of Interventions through Key Stages 1–4

This chapter takes the form of a selection of case studies which together demonstrate the range of ways in which dyspraxia may impact upon educational attainments, daily living, social and emotional development and behaviour. The case studies span all four key stages in order to explore the different challenges which the infant, junior and secondary phases of education present for an individual with dyspraxia, and the types of strategies which have supported the children within their mainstream school settings.

Introduction

The children described are mostly at the School Action Plus stage of the Code of Practice and the two who do have a statement of special educational needs require the delivery of speech and language therapy and physiotherapy programmes in school. Most of the children can be well supported by judicious management of the physical and social environment, and the delivery of the curriculum.

The individual recommendations for support in school will be guided not only by the needs of the individual as ascertained as a result of the full multi-agency assessment but also by the demands of the curriculum at their key stage. A model devised from the work of Gary La Vigna is a useful framework within which to consider any individual recommendations. He suggests that it is helpful to address:

(a) modifications to the learning environment and the physical environment;
(b) the teaching of new skills;
(c) support in the form of coping strategies.

A simple example for a child who had difficulties with handwriting might involve:

(a) lesson notes as an alternative to copying, and provision of a writing slope;
(b) teaching handwriting patterns initially large scale on a vertical surface;
(c) provision of a scribe for written tasks which have a focus on content.

As a child moves through the key stages, the emphasis on achieving new skills versus teaching coping strategies may change as illustrated in Figure 7.1. The recommendations for each of the children described in the case studies follows the model.

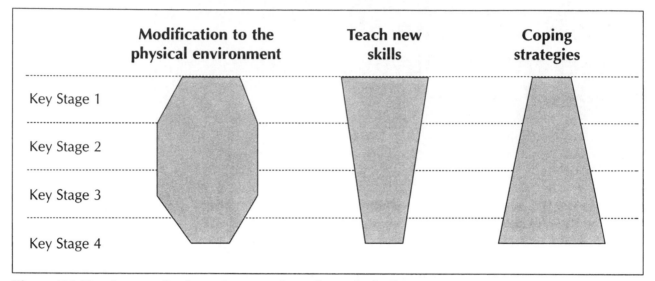

Figure 7.1 Varying emphasis on interventions through the key stages

CASE STUDY 12 Key Stage 1

C, Year 1

C, age 5 years 8 months has oral and verbal dyspraxic difficulties which were diagnosed when he was 4 years old. His profile suggests language as well as articulatory and oral skill problems, with the added complication of poor fine- and gross-motor coordination. C also experiences some difficulties with feeding.
  Currently he:

- cannot produce the following sounds in isolation: 's, z, th, th, she, zh (as in leisure), ch, j, r and y';
- can sequence individual consonant sounds learned, but needs further work on CVC strings (consonant+vowel+consonant);
- has learned all vowels except diphthongs and triphthongs;
- has difficulties with oral skills movements involving rapid movements of his lips and tongue;
- continues to experience difficulties with breath control. His voice is either too soft or too loud;
- has poor phonological awareness for syllable and rhyme. He cannot easily discriminate speech sounds in words or predict the correct sound in a word;
- has great difficulty with the language of space and time;
- has poor word order;
- is becoming an isolated child.

Modifications to the physical environment

- Choose a likely child to befriend him and to act as an interpreter as and when needed.
- Give access to a large mirror, preferably in a quiet room in the school.
- Provide a classroom assistant to help as and when directed/needed in class, and work on specific activities provided by the speech and language therapist.
- Acquire materials for an oral skills box in collaboration with the speech and language therapist.

New skills

- Expand the number of consonant sounds, working specifically with 's' and 'z'.
- Learn a range of CV strings and CCC strings, using speech sounds already learned.
- Learn sequences of lip and tongue movements plus breath-control exercises, using the time in group work on these skills to include work on social skills, e.g. turn taking, good sitting, no interrupting, requesting appropriately.
- Teach 'long/short' precise word meanings with real things, lines, environment sounds, musical sounds, speech sounds.
- Teach the precise word meanings for 'noisy/quiet', using the children themselves, environmental sounds, musical instruments, speech sounds.
- Teach word order through reading/writing sessions in class and/or as part of the literacy hour.
- Use opportunities to teach language of space and time in PE, class routines, project work and maths.
- Teach social skills throughout the day and specifically in circle time and withdrawal group.
- Teach feeding skills in individual sessions, as part of social skills/oral skills group and at lunchtime.

Coping strategies

- Cueing (suggest Jane Passey's system) is useful for teaching other children who have difficulties with reading. In-service training will be needed. Alternatively, a system of cues based on Letterland can be used, particularly for consonants.
- Use Letterland and/or the Nuffield symbols.
- Use the Makaton signing system and symbols.
- Use a visual timetable.
- Picture Exchange Communication System (PECS) could be used if the child has become selectively mute.
- The colour coding of words using a 'Breakthrough' approach can be useful for children with literacy difficulties.
- Use symbols or pictures around the room to help the child understand where things are and how s/he can access them.
- All children in the class have a target of their own to remember for the week or month. In this way the child with dyspraxia will

not be made to feel too different if s/he has several targets to work on every day.

- Use an egg timer or similar device to help the child understand the passing of time.
- The classroom assistant or another child can help to interpret for the child.
- Use 'forced alternatives' in order to assist the staff to understand the child.
- Use pictures as cues for all the class to remind them that they need to have 'good sitting, good looking, no interruptions and taking turns'.
- Have a home/school book – it helps enormously with 'News Time' and in this way the child with dyspraxia can make a contribution.
- Have a chart for achievement. Encourage the child to participate in 'Good Work' assemblies.
- Use social skills and/or oral skills groups to improve the child's tolerance of eating foods of various textures. As a rule, it is helpful to introduce food liked/tolerated with food the child dislikes or won't attempt to eat.
- Encourage the child to take messages but always write these down and let a friend go with them.

CASE STUDY 13 KEY STAGE 1

N, Year 2

N, 7 years 1 month, in mainstream school with statemented provision. N has been assessed as having average cognitive ability but the dyspraxia affects fine-motor skills, including speech clarity when he is excited, and gross-motor skills.

Modifications to the environment

- OT advice about posture and seating arrangements;
- table and chair size adapted to his needs or provision of a footstool;
- a beanbag for carpet time (unable to maintain balance when seated on the floor) and assembly;
- a sloping board for pencil and paper activities;
- a triangle grip on the pencil;
- short learning targets with opportunities for legitimate breaks (finds it hard to sustain effort, especially on pencil and paper activities);
- he does not require extra support in PE or have difficulties on the playground; other children may need more help in these areas.

New skills

- support to follow his physiotherapy programme in school;

- support to follow his speech and language therapy programme in school;
- listening to stories to provide a model of formal grammatical English for the organisation of his expressive language (grammar and phonology immature);
- learning to read will support the maturation of language form;
- teaching handwriting skills;
- provide activities to develop bilateral integration and strength of grip;
- a drawing programme.

Coping strategies

- reminders to slow down when he is excited as speech becomes difficult to follow;
- use of the computer for recording and some learning tasks ('Clicker' software is helpful);
- use of line guides to help visual scanning of a text (the cursor on the computer screen provides a spatial location cue).

CASE STUDY 14 Key Stage 2

E, Year 5

E, 9 years 3 months in mainstream school at School Action Plus. Average verbal ability but Performance Scale Score at 1st centile. Learning style showed difficulties with:

- impulsive approach to problem solving;
- focusing of visual and auditory attention;
- high levels of anxiety, low levels of confidence;
- monitoring her performance on most tasks;
- chaotic handwriting.

Modifications to the physical environment

- support for organisation by use of visual timetable with symbols chosen by her;
- flow chart for task organisation;
- cue cards for gathering equipment;
- short tasks with achieveable targets to ensure maximum experience of success as a learner;
- rewards for success.

New skills

- handwriting programme;
- keyboard skills (learning will take longer for her);
- social skills training to develop verbal and non-verbal aspects of communication.

- development of independent writing by providing short, differentiated, structured tasks and rewards for task completion;
- support for OT programme in school;
- use of writing frames (Maureen Lewis and David Wray).

Coping strategies

- access to alternative means of recording – scribe, tape recorder – when the task focus is on content;
- use of verbal mediation to help focus attention on a task and to organise a task;
- a procedure for monitoring and evaluating each product;
- support to enhance self-esteem.

CASE STUDY 15 Key Stage 3

P, Year 8

P, 12 years 4 months (National Curriculum Year 8), mainstream school at School Action Plus. Dyspraxia affects coordination, sensory processing, balance, speed and fluency of movement. Handwriting and the organisation/coordination required for practical subjects were his main concerns. WISC III UK Verbal Abilities were at 86th centile but he scored below average for Performance Scale Tests except for Picture Completion (minimal motor response). Reading was at 16th centile and some problems with scanning and convergence were noted.

Modifications to the physical environment

- access to word processing facilities and a graphics package to support the production of diagrams, graphs and technical designs;
- enlargement of worksheets and other written material as appropriate (problems with small-sized print);
- provision of an amanuensis in practical lessons for which safety may be an issue;
- a sloping surface for writing.

New skills

- instruction in touch-typing and access to instruction tapes;
- use of a graphics program on the computer;
- techniques which minimise the need for verbatim recording, e.g. using flow diagrams, mind maps, dictaphone.

Coping strategies

- in-class support for note-taking: lesson notes in advance for highlighting or provided by LSA;

- use of the techniques which minimise the need for writing *per se*;
- extended time or adjusted targets for the completion of written assignments;
- ideas for the support of task organisation.

CASE STUDY 16 Key Stage 4

G, Year 10

G, aged 14 years 2 months, National Curriculum Year 10, mainstream school at School Action Plus. A late diagnosis of dyspraxia at age 9 years. Some residual oral-verbal dyspraxia but very high verbal abilities and Reading Age at 91st centile, spelling at 86th centile. Handwriting a major problem.

Modifications to the physical environment

- support in practical sessions for science and technology (soldering for electronics was particularly a problem);
- access to word processor at lunchtime (he often did homework then as a preference to going outside).

New skills

- typing practice to improve speed;
- teach mind mapping, key-wording techniques.

Coping strategies

- use of word processor for homework, lessons, examination assignments;
- alternatives to note-taking or copying from the board or a text to include a personal shorthand, key-wording, mind mapping, lesson notes in advance, LSA to take notes;
- extra time to complete written assignments and tests/ examinations;
- spatial aspects of assignments supported by use of stencils, provision of templates of diagrams, maps, etc. for labelling only; use of software such as Pictures for Projects;
- consideration for special arrangements for GCSE examinations.

Chapter 8

Activities to Develop Motor Skills and Self-esteem

This chapter relies heavily on the work of Peter Cartlidge, PE specialist and one-time deputy head teacher in Brighton. In 1987 Cartlidge asked the Year 3 and 4 teachers at his school to nominate their most clumsy children to take part in an intervention programme. The initiative was prompted by the question: 'Mum, why do they pick me last?' (Cartlidge 1995), and by an awareness of the impact that clumsiness may have upon self-esteem and subsequently upon behaviour:

> The child with low self-esteem will lack confidence in his ability to succeed, consequently he may try to avoid situations that he perceives as potentially humiliating. To be punished and, perhaps, be seen as something of a hero by their peers is better than being seen as foolish.
>
> (Laurence, *Enhancing Self-esteem in the Classroom* in Cartlidge 1995)

The group started with six children in 1987 and formed a pilot study for what became known as the Esteem Club. The original group sessions were all planned in collaboration with the local occupational therapy team. Many of the children involved in the subsequent groups had had an occupational therapy assessment and an occupational therapist was always available as a consultant to the group programme. By 1998 over 200 children in East Sussex had benefited from the programme

For ten years, the Esteem Club recruited children from many different schools in the county. The children were identified by means of a checklist (see Appendix IV), and attended for a series of ten weekly sessions after school. Most were transported by their parents, who were invited to stay and observe the sessions so that they could practise some of the skills at home. During each session the children carried out a range of activities designed to develop particular aspects of motor skill. The sessions lasted 45 minutes and ended with circle time in which the children discussed how they were progressing and set new personal targets. The effectiveness of the training was measured by means of questionnaires, feedback from teachers, parents and the children themselves.

The checklist, Appendix IV, was used to identify particular areas of strength and weakness, and the intervention programme was planned to address particular areas of need.

The apparatus used during the sessions was simple and readily available in most schools, and the gymnasium was used for all the activities. The children were not required to be in full PE kit which might, because of past experiences, have triggered a defensive approach to the sessions. Instead, they were encouraged to wear tracksuit bottoms and no shoes or socks. Activities were broken into small steps and chaining forwards, or backwards, helped to ensure that the children experienced success.

The training was based on a pyramid model of coordination, within which each physical or sensory component is interrelated. The complete pyramid is seen as a strong structure of interwoven features which contribute to efficient motor performance.

The Motor Skills Training Programme

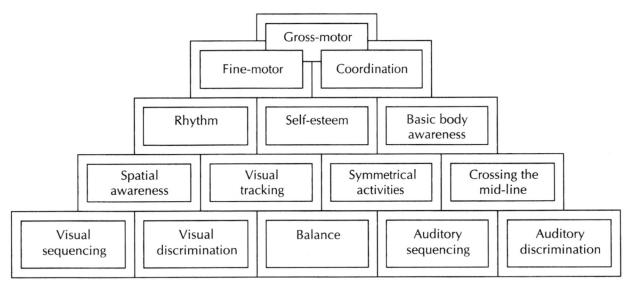

Figure 8.1 The pyramid model of coordination

Specific activities can be targeted at each block of the pyramid:

Activities directed to specific difficulties.

1. Gross-motor skills
   - *wrestling – body and arm
   - *pushing
   - *pulling
   - aerobic exercises and dance routines
   - many conventional PE activities with the skill level adapted to ensure the success of the participants.

   * to support the concept of the control of the force of movement.

2. Fine-motor skills	• finger games, involving independent finger movements • finger strength promotion, e.g. putting pegs on a line, threading beads, peg patterns, posting activities, pencil and paper activities, 'feely' bags, tool manipulation, e.g. using scissors.
3. Coordination	• 'mirror' shapes • winding thread, winding up a weight on string tied to a baton • dot-to-dot • mazes • stepping over, stepping under • going through hoops etc. • dance routines, especially those using baton manipulation as an integral feature • most conventional PE activities graded to ensure the success of the participants • line-dancing routines address whole-body movements and awareness, mid-line work, balance, sequencing and memory, as well as providing for some symmetrical activity routines.
4. Rhythm	• any musical activity • switch • hopping • jumping • skipping • dance routines.
5. Basic body movements and awareness	• run – with changes of speed and direction. The concepts of fast/slow movements may need specific work for children with dyspraxia/DCD • jump – many variations are possible • stretch and relax, stretch and curl • dressing up games – these also involve balance, spatial awareness, and mid-line work.
6. Spatial awareness	• language work using the concepts of space • whole-body movement or placing objects relative to the body or

other objects using language such as over/under, in front/behind, left/right, etc.
- moving behind or placing objects in front
- roll from here to there
- jump in a shape
- object search games which may also help with organisational skills.

7. Visual tracking
- jump ball or rope
- throwing
- catching
- following moving objects
- search puzzles and mazes as found in child activity books.

8. Symmetrical activities
- mirror shapes
- right and left identification using object placing and whole-body work
- skipping
- dance routines especially the 'cheer leader' variety which have baton manipulation as a component
- a body board (like a large skateboard) on which children lie prone and propel themselves using the arms. Simple backward and forward movement is a prelude to steering around obstacle courses of varying complexity.

9. Mid-line work
- 'Simon says'
- left/right work
- as above, eyes closed.

10. Visual sequencing/memory
- pattern copying
- coloured bead threading
- shape and size puzzles
- recalling objects on a tray
- card games.

11. Visual discrimination
- matching card games
- spot the difference using picture material
- snap
- lotto
- dominoes
- odd one out

	• object sorting with varying degrees of difficulty to which a time challenge might be added.
12. Balance	• any static display • walking on a line, balance beam, etc. • running with direction changes • leaning and balancing on either leg.
13. Auditory sequential memory	• 'Switch' rhythms • moving to specific rhythms • shopping lists • recall of number or word sequences.
14. Auditory discrimination/integrity	• identifying sounds • locating sounds • yes/no questions • true/false questions • same or different.
15. Self-esteem	• any of the activities carried out in a supportive environment where the child experiences success will help to build self-esteem.

Lesson plans for five sessions of the Esteem Club

Lesson 1

Introduction

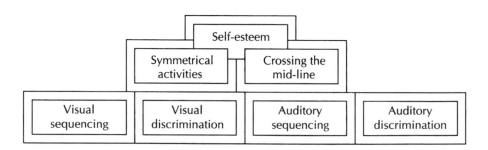

1. Rocking	Rocking in time to music or a drumbeat may be carried out while standing or sitting. It may involve the children holding hands in a circle or sitting with both hands on the shoulders of the child in front. A variant on rocking might take the form of a Mexican Wave.

2. Coin manipulation

This fine-motor activity might involve picking up and posting coins, quickly passing coins round a circle using a pincer grip, spinning coins or sorting coins.

3. Tiddlywinks

The size of the target and whether it has raised sides will change the skill level of this game.

Main development

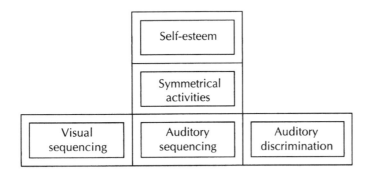

1. Ladder games

The ladder may be a real ladder or squares marked on the floor with masking tape. Raising the ladder above floor level and setting individual targets may be used to vary the level of challenge.

2. Tunnelling

Sheets, blankets, mats and tarpaulins can all be used to create tunnels. Tunnels may be made from hoops and suitable material.

3. Rolling along a mat

Lateral rolling (log rolls) would come before any attempts at formal forward rolls etc.

4. Bottoms

This is most safely undertaken on a trampoline but the soft landing mats used for PE may also be used. The children stand still and then drop onto their bottom on the soft surface. It is a confidence-building activity as well as a physical one.

5. Balance bar

The difficulty of the challenge is determined by the height and width of the bar. Support may be needed initially at any new stage and be withdrawn gradually.

6. Toe exercises

These may involve walking on tip-toe or exercises which involve flexible control such as picking up objects with the toes, passing objects to others using toes, walking while holding objects, such as coins, between the toes. A 'toe tray' may be assembled with a selection of suitable objects which are picked up using the toes. This may be timed for setting personal targets, or be incorporated as a team relay activity.

Conclusion

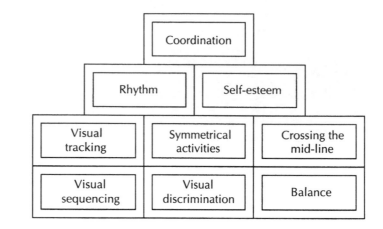

1. Recalling numbers

This class of activities is described in many books about auditory memory. The recall of numbers, or words, can be done in small groups so that:

Child A says a number
Child B says that number and adds another etc.
When a child fails to repeat the sequence, the chain starts again.

Small groups are best at first so that everyone has several turns and feels successful. The larger the group, the longer the potential number chains and the fewer the opportunities for individuals to feel successful.

2. Chains of command

These may be cumulative as with the recall of numbers so that:

Child A tells Child B to do (i)
Child B carries out their task and tells Child C to do that and another task.

Alternative chains of command are 'Chinese whispers' activities.

3. Language work

The language to do with spatial concepts is often difficult for children with motor-coordination problems. Any activities which involve placing objects relative to the body or another object, can reinforce the language of space, direction and distance. Above, below, behind are early spatial concepts. The language of body parts can also be reinforced in this context. The work may involve the whole body (gross-motor skills). Children move over/under, left/right, position themselves behind/in front, next to a fixed point, according to the directions of the leader.

Alternatively, the children may kneel on a mat and move an object such as a beanbag in front/behind, left/right, to the side, above/below, next to, using their own body as the reference point. Crossing the mid-line and symmetrical activities can be targeted in this way.

The level of challenge can be changed by the vocabulary used and by introducing more than one object to manipulate.

4. Parachute

A familiar, cooperative game with which to finish the session, before the de-briefing and target setting.

Lesson 2

Introduction

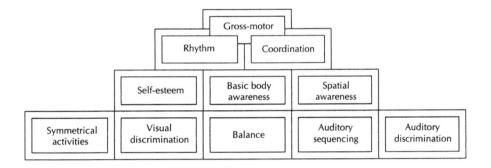

1. Circles; clapping

This exercise may be carried out standing, sitting or kneeling. The clapping may involve just one person clapping their hands in imitation of the leader; above their head, behind or in front of their body, to each side, under each leg raised in turn, etc. The language of space, position and body parts can be reinforced during the activity.

Clapping may involve pairs of students in clapping games which are still familiar on some playgrounds, e.g. clap together (own hands), clap together (partner's hands), right on right clap, left on left clap, etc. The clapping sequences can be varied to make them more complex and a time element may add a further dimension.

2. Shopping list

This is one form of the class of auditory memory games which are often played in the classroom: *I went to the supermarket and I bought ...*

Other variations may involve naming specialist shops, e.g. sports shops or packing 'grandmother's trunk' or 'my case to go on holiday'. *(See also Lesson 1, C No. 1)*

Note: When activities are cross-referenced between lessons
I = Introduction
MD = Main development
C = Conclusion

3. Rhythms

These may involve clapping, rocking *(See Lesson 1, I No. 1)* or using musical instruments. Dance rhythms and routines will add a gross-motor skill component and are fun warm-up exercises.

4. Stars

This involves stepping in and out, over a prone body.

Main development

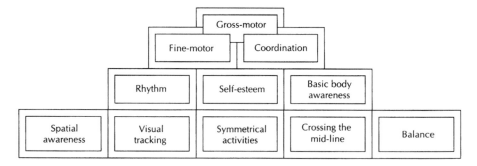

1. Over and under canes

The canes may be held by other members of the group as well as being part of the set apparatus. The heights of the canes and the number of elements can be adjusted to vary the skill level of the activity.

2. Balance – bench raised

(See also Balance in Lesson 1, MD No. 5)
For some children, the first step towards achieving this target would be to

develop confidence 'walking the line', i.e. a line on the ground marked with masking tape. The bench raising should take place gradually and with the child in control of the degree of challenge.

3. Pegs and string

A game of pegging out the washing using a variety of 'odd' garments can be great fun as a team activity. More control may be needed for smaller pegs to be placed on, for example, the rim of a container, or when attempting to peg together several different pieces of paper/card/material, etc.

4. Backward and forward rolling

(See Lesson 1, MD No. 3)

5. Beanbag guiding

This is an early prelude to learning to guide a ball with a stick (e.g. for hockey) or dribbling a ball (for football). The obstacle course for guiding the beanbag may be made as simple or complex as is appropriate.

6. Bench pull along

An exercise which is good for upper body strength and for symmetrical movement development. The child lies face down on the bench and uses both arms to pull him/herself to the end of the bench.

7. Rolling on a mat

(See also Lesson 1, MD No. 3)

8. Hoops – hopping

The hoops are placed on the ground at various distances apart, depending on the challenge level of the activity. Some children may need to start with a more simple activity such as hoop jumping with feet together; others may need to perfect their hopping technique before this task is introduced.

Conclusion

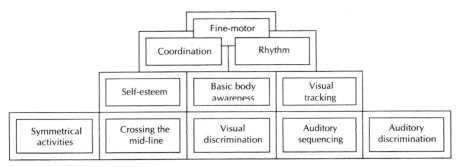

1. Separate hand functions	This activity would usually be carried out with the group imitating the actions of the group leader or in pairs with children taking it in turns to model and to copy. Other possibilities include picking up and placing small objects using games such as 'pick a stick', peg board patterns, posting activities, extracting coins from playdoh balls, pressing buttons with individual fingers to make sounds, etc.
2. Visual tracking	Follow the finger movements of a partner with eyes and head movement as they make patterns in the air. Following the point of light from a pencil torch on the wall in a darkened room may serve as a whole-group variation. Children may also practise moving their eyes to follow the target while trying to keep their head still. Children with ocular dyspraxia may find this very hard to achieve. Other classroom activities such as maze drawing, picture searches (e.g. 'Where's Wally?' books) and even reading itself, all promote visual-motor control.
3. Mid-line work with eyes open and shut	These activities will involve children crossing the mid-line with their preferred and non-preferred hands to pick up objects using visual or tactile cues.
4. Relaxing	Relaxation activities are as powerful with children as they are with adults. The usual format is to tense and relax particular parts of the body, e.g. hands or toes, or even muscle groups, e.g. calf or stomach muscles. The tension can be reinforced by an ingoing breath and the relaxation enhanced by breathing out slowly. Once various parts of the body have been tensed and relaxed in turn, a further relaxation can be encouraged by the group leader talking about parts of the body, e.g. arms/head 'feeling heavy'. Involving a relaxing visual image of a favourite quiet place can also enhance the feelings of stillness, calm and relaxation. Relaxation is a useful activity at the start of a session if children are 'high',

for example when coming in after play, as well as at the conclusion of a demanding series of activities.

Lesson 3

Introduction

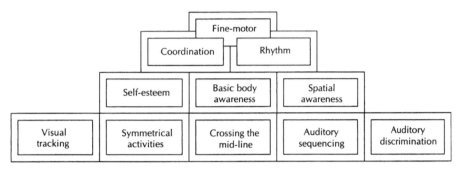

| | | | |
| 1. Buzz | Adult starts the games by clicking fingers and calling out someone's name. That person then clicks and calls out another name. The idea is to speed up the responses as the group gets more experienced. |

| 2. Sticks | A variation on the family game of 'Pick a Stick'. The sticks can be more robust for children who have difficulty with a steady pincer grip and finger separation. A collection of pencils would be less delicate than the 'sticks' used in commercial versions of the game. |

| 3. Mirrors | The children work in pairs, taking it in turns to lead. The second child mirrors the movements of their partner. |

| 4. Feely bag | Any suitable sized objects might be put in a feely bag. These could be random or follow a theme, e.g. all toy plastic animals. This activity is useful for developing proprioception and the efficient interpretation of the sensory input from touch. |

| 5. Language work | *(See Lesson 1, C No. 3)*
The directions used are spatial concepts which children with motor difficulties may find hard to understand or to translate into action, i.e. control the execution of their motor plan. |

Main development

```
                    ┌─────────────────────┐
                    │     Gross-motor     │
              ┌─────┴───────┬─────────────┴───┐
              │  Fine-motor │  Coordination   │
        ┌─────┴──────┬──────┴──────┬──────────┴──────┐
        │   Rhythm   │ Self-esteem │   Basic body    │
        │            │             │   awareness     │
   ┌────┴───┬────────┼─────────────┼──────────┬───────┴───┐
   │ Visual │ Spatial│ Symmetrical │ Crossing │           │
   │tracking│awareness│ activities │ the      │  Balance  │
   │        │        │             │ mid-line │           │
   └────────┴────────┴─────────────┴──────────┴───────────┘
```

1. Stepping over canes

   (See Lesson 2, MD No. 1)

2. Beanbag guiding

   (See Lesson 2, MD No. 5)

3. Pulling up a bench and sliding down

   This work on a sloping bench builds on the activity in Lesson 2, MD No. 6.

4. Hoops

   Hoops can be used in many floor exercises, including their use as stepping stones. The distances between the hoops and direction changes can be used to vary the level of difficulty *(see also Lesson 2, MD No. 8)*.

5. Rolling

   There are many variations on this activity *(see Lesson 1, MD No. 3)*.

6. Mat with quoits beneath

   This can be a diving for treasure game. The children take it in turns to go under the mat and retrieve a quoit. Smaller target objects would add difficulty to the activity. Alternatively, the quoits can be used as stepping stones, with children feeling for the quoits with their feet as they 'cross the river'.

7. Toe exercises

   (See Lesson 1, MD No. 6)

8. Skipping

   A self-explanatory activity which can be done as an individual or a group activity using familiar playground skipping games. For boys – remember that footballers and other athletes skip as part of their fitness routines.

Conclusion

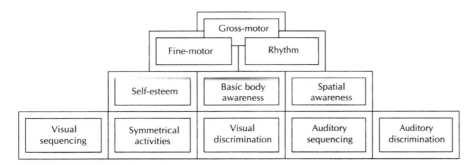

1. Switch	Clapping activities where the group has to watch the leader and follow when they change
	    – the rhythm
	    – the clapping movement, e.g. hands together to clapping hands on knees
	    – to partner clapping.
	(See Lesson 2, I No. 1)

2. Missing object tray	This visual spatial memory game has many different names. Essentially, the leader takes one or more objects away from the tray and the children guess which one is missing. The game may also offer the opportunity to check and extend vocabulary. The objects on the tray may be concept themed, e.g. shapes, model vehicles, etc.
3. Threading beads in a sequence	This activity explains itself, and the patterns can be simple (alternating colours or shapes) and build in complexity, e.g. a four colour/shape repeating sequence. The motor element of the task can be made more challenging by reduction of the thickness of the thread and the size of the beads. Peg patterns can be used in a similar way to promote spatial awareness and manual dexterity.
4. Duck, duck and goose	The children sit in a circle and the start player goes round the outside of the circle touching the children lightly on the shoulder. As s/he does this they say 'duck' until, at a point of their choosing, they say 'goose' and run back to their

place in the circle. The child tapped as 'goose' tries to get back to the place of the first child before them. If they do not achieve this, they become the active player.

5. 'Simon says'/'O'Grady says'

A good activity for working on the language of body parts and sequence of instructions which involve carrying out a motor plan. This familiar game may be played at many levels of challenge.

Lesson 4

Introduction

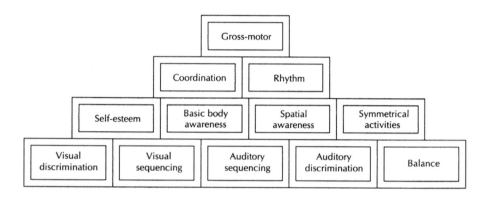

1. Rocking

(See Lesson 1, I No. 1)

2. Noise bag

A noise bag is similar to a feely bag but the contents all make a noise, e.g. packing wrap that 'pops', squeaky toys, etc. The active player makes a sound using the objects and the rest of the group guess the object. This is helpful in developing auditory attention and auditory discrimination.

3. Playing cards

Any suitable game will promote manual dexterity and some, such as 'snap' based games, help to speed up reaction times. Visual discrimination is involved in any matching games.

4. Running

This is another variant on following spatial directions but on this occasion a clap is the signal rather than the words themselves. It may be hard for children to listen for the clap, recall the code and carry out the appropriate movements. Starting from a stationary position with 1 clap = 1 step forward, 2 claps = 1 step back, may be appropriate as a first stage and the game can be gradually made more demanding.

The complete code might be:

1 clap = run forward
2 claps = run back
3 claps = side, right
4 claps = side, left.

5. Stars   *(See Lesson 2, I No. 4)*

6. Jump rope   This may be familiar as part of a skipping game. The stationary rope is gradually raised, but children should volunteer for each new level of difficulty to avoid experiences of failure *(see also Lesson 3, MD No. 8)*.

Main development

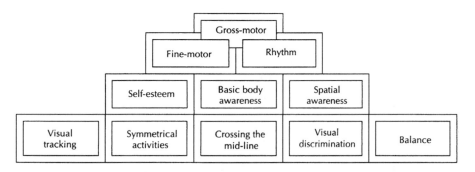

1. Hoops and beanbag steering

These hoops are the croquet hoop variety rather than hoola-hoops laid on the ground as in Lesson 2, MD No. 8. The 'goals' add variety to beanbag activities as in Lesson 2, MD No. 5.

2. Climbing frame

A self-explanatory activity, but one which children with coordination difficulties may find challenging and try to avoid in a PE lesson. Experience shows that in a small, supportive group they are much more likely to test their personal competence and set realistic personal targets.

3. Maze work

A maze can be constructed from any available apparatus, e.g. chairs, cones or ropes. Navigating the maze may be an aim itself, but variations can be considered. For example, Child A gives Child B (blindfolded or not) detailed instructions of how to go through the maze

'Take 2 steps forward. Turn left. Take 2 steps to the right', etc.

4. Sloping balance	*(See Lesson 2, MD No. 2)*
5. Rolling	*(See Lesson 2, MD Nos 4 and 7)*
6. Pegs on string or cups	*(See Lesson 2, MD No. 3)*
7. Hoops and ropes	An obstacle course may be set up, using hoops and ropes. Children go through hoops and under/over ropes. The challenge can be varied according to the number of the obstacles and other parameters such as the size of the hoops.

Conclusion

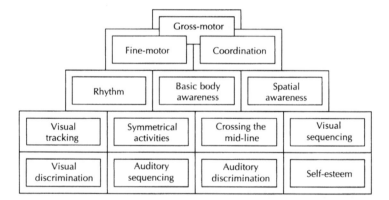

1. Tearing paper	A starting point may simply be the tearing of paper into strips – more advanced origami activities may follow.
2. Copying movements	This may be a form of mirror work *(see Lesson 3, I No. 3)* or visual tracking *(see Lesson 2, C No. 2)*. If the eyes are shut, the follower keeps physical contact with the hand of the leading child.
3. Threading bead sequences	*(See Lesson 3, C No. 3)*
4. Language instructions	Spatial and body part language is particularly relevant *(see Lesson 1, C No. 3 and Lesson 3, I No. 5)*.

5. Tag

A rather boisterous finish to this session and some relaxation may be needed before the feedback and target setting can take place.

Lesson 5

Introduction

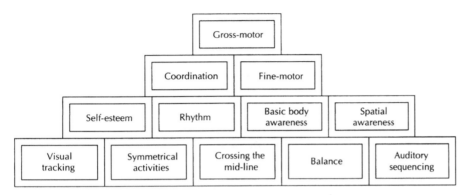

1. Rhythm work

(See Lesson 2, I No. 3)

2. Target practice

This activity may involve any size of projectile and any size of container. Balloons and beanbags are relatively slow moving for the early stages of practice. Large, soft balls are a development while small hard balls and small targets, e.g. throwing through a quoit, require high levels of skill. Both throwing and kicking activities might be incorporated into target practice.

3. Catching

The progression of the materials used is as for target practice. It may help some children to practise 'batting' a balloon as Stage 1. This will allow them to concentrate on watching the projectile, i.e. visual tracking, without having to organise the movements for catching at the same time.

Tracking Practice: Simplest Level: as a prelude to developing catching skills, 'Batting a balloon'.

Gradually introduce objects which move faster, e.g. a large soft ball → smaller rubber ball. Once a child can track a target moving towards him/her and not close their eyes, it is appropriate to move on to catching practice *per se*.

Catching Practice: Simplest Level:

a. Adult thrower stands within arms' length and throws a balloon or large soft ball, slowly, so that the child has time to watch the ball and organise the catching movement.

Progression:

b. Adult gradually increases the distance.
c. Adult uses a faster moving ball.
d. Adult uses a smaller ball in stages.

For some groups of children, a catching and throwing activity may be important to incorporate into each lesson plan.

4. Jump rope

(See Lesson 4, I No. 6)

Main development

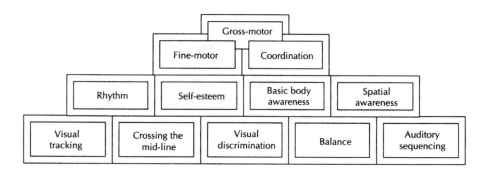

1. Balance bar

(See Lesson 1, MD No. 5)

2. Suspended bench

These activities are discussed in Lesson 2, MD 2.

3. Rolling

(See Lesson 1, MD No. 3)

4. Mazes

(See Lesson 4, MD No. 3)

5. Tunnel pull

Tunnelling activities are discussed in Lesson 3, MD No. 6. This variation involves Child A pulling Child B through the tunnel.

6. Rope maze

(See Lesson 4, MD No. 3)

7. Hoops

(See Lesson 2, MD No. 8)

Conclusion

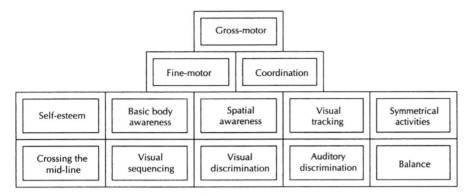

		Gross-motor		
	Fine-motor		Coordination	
Self-esteem	Basic body awareness	Spatial awareness	Visual tracking	Symmetrical activities
Crossing the mid-line	Visual sequencing	Visual discrimination	Auditory discrimination	Balance

1. Jump into a ...   (Square, circle, triangle, rectangle, etc.) The shapes may be solid ones or marked on the floor with masking tape, or be marked with chalk. At the verbal command, children jump into a named shape.

2. Threading beads   *(See Lesson 3, C No. 3)*

3. Chains of command   *(See Lesson 1, C No. 2)*

4. Leg, tunnel, ball   A ball is rolled through a tunnel of legs. The last child in line picks up the ball, runs to the front of the line and rolls the ball through the leg tunnel.

5. Tearing paper   *(See Lesson 4, C No. 1)*

6. Relaxing   *(See Lesson 2, C No. 4)*

Summary

Five lesson plans have been presented in detail so that a range of activities might be described.

The lesson plans which are presented in this section are only one model, and group leaders may find it more appropriate to mix and match the activities according to the needs of the children in their group. The general principles for planning an activity session are:

- to start with a series of warm-up activities;
- to plan the main development with a balance of activities which are appropriate to the needs of the children in the group;
- to conclude with a selection of team building, less active games and relaxation. The conclusion of the lesson plans 3 and 4 do not follow this general principle and thought should be given to the order of the activities if the lesson plans presented in this section are followed;
- to end the session with group evaluation, praise and personal target setting.

Since the original group was assembled in 1987, many other teachers and special needs coordinators in the south-east of England have set up their own Esteem Clubs to serve the needs of individual schools or clusters of schools. The help of the local occupational therapy teams has always been sought in setting up the groups and advising about the content of the sessions. The groups have proved popular with parents and the children.

The participants have the chance to develop their physical skills in a supportive, non-judgemental setting as a member of a group of children who are at similar skill levels. The individual target setting and personal evaluation in the plenary session are important elements in the process of raising self-esteem. Before and after questionnaires for teachers report positive changes in basic physical skills, confidence to participate in class-based physical activities and improved peer relationships among the children who have attended the Esteem Clubs.

Other sources of information about school-based programmes

The Right to Movement by David Stewart

This book includes a survey of programmes which are commonly used in schools, and many ideas for activities which are similar to those used in the Esteem Club.

The activities are grouped as:

1. Tags
   Chase and release games which help to develop reaction times and energy levels. Examples include:

   - *Stuck in the mud*
     When caught, the child must stand with legs apart until another child crawls through his/her legs to release him/her.
   - *Chain tag*
     Start with two children holding hands. Each child who is caught joins the chain – an exhausting game this one – until there is only one child left. He or she can then pick a forfeit for everyone else.

2. Relationship games
   These help to develop cooperation and the control of the force of movement. Examples include:

   - *Back to back*
     Here the children sit back to back on the floor, feet and hands spread, and on the command 'Go!' attempt to push each other backwards. It is a competitive and strong activity.

   - *Starfish*
     Child A lies face down on the floor and tries to stick to it. Child B has to pull the starfish over on to its back. Change over.

3. Rhyme and rhythm
   These games include finger action games, songs and rounds.

4. Motor skill circuits

The circuits can be adapted to the individual needs and skills of the children. The circuits start very simply by moving between two mats in a straight line in a variety of ways, e.g. hopping, skipping. Obstacles are gradually introduced, e.g. hoops to go through or apparatus to go under or over.

The next phase of the activity is to introduce more apparatus and new directions in which to travel. A simple skills circuit is shown in Figure 8.2.

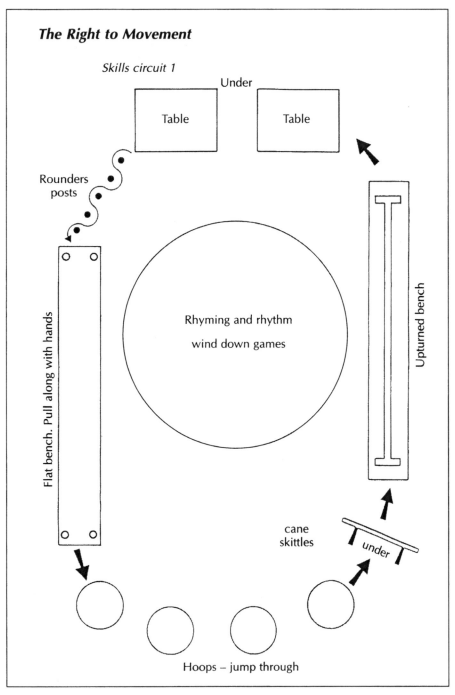

Figure 8.2 A simple skills circuit (from Stewart 1990)

5. Memory and sequencing activities
   These can include team games and memory games such as 'Simon says'.

Graded Activities for Children with Motor Difficulties by James Russell

There are 14 programmes in this book which involve three groups of activity.

1. Gross-motor skills:	Gross-motor control and coordination Gross-motor control – walking and running Dynamic balance programme Balancing on one foot, hopping and skipping Catching a ball Throwing, striking and kicking a ball Jumping.
2. Sensory integration and body awareness:	Body awareness through tactile feedback Knowledge of left and right Activities involving movement from left to right.
3. Visual-motor skills:	Visual discrimination Visual tracking Activities for the 'writing' hand Establishing handwriting patterns.

Motor Development

Run without falling
Kick a ball if standing
Throw a ball – inaccurately
Walk sideways and backwards
Turn around
Jump with both feet
Catch ball – bring it into body   2–3 years

Walk on tip-toes
Ride a tricycle
Stand on one foot momentarily
Jump up high
Go upstairs with alternate feet
Catch a large ball   3–4 years

Jump a distance
Balance 4–6 seconds
Come downstairs alternate feet
Skip first attempt
Hop first attempt
Catch ball (using arms more than hands)   4–5 years
Jump over small object

Balance 8 seconds
Hop
Skip rhythmically
Heel walking
Bounce and catch a ball
Jump up to knee height   5–6 years

Toss, bounce, catch ball
Crawl around obstacle course
Throw at a target
Bounce ball and catch with one hand
Jump rope
Balance 15 seconds (10 secs eyes closed)   6–7 years

Overview of the Developmental Stages for Achieving Pencil Control

Stage	1	Scribbles randomly
Stage	2 a	Scribbles spontaneously in a horizontal direction
	b	Scribbles spontaneously in a vertical direction
	c	Scribbles spontaneously in a circular direction
Stage	3 a	Imitates a horizontal scribble direction
	b	Imitates a vertical scribble direction
	c	Imitates a circular scribble direction
Stage	4 a	Imitates a horizontal line
	b	Imitates a vertical line
	c	Imitates a circular line
Stage	5 a	Copies a horizontal line
	b	Copies a vertical line
	c	Copies a circle
Stage	6 a	Imitates a cross
	b	Copies a cross
Stage	7 a	Imitates a right – left diagonal /
	b	Copies a right – left diagonal /
Stage	8 a	Imitates a square
	b	Copies a square
Stage	9 a	Imitates a left – right diagonal \
	b	Copies a left – right diagonal \
Stage	10 a	Imitates an oblique cross X
	b	Copies an oblique cross X
Stage	11 a	Imitates a triangle
	b	Copies a triangle
Stage	12 a	Imitates a diamond
	b	Copies a diamond

NOTE: Imitate – Teacher draws the shape, child watches, child draws the shape.
Copy – Teacher gives child a drawing of the shape, child copies the shape.

Appendix III

Handwriting Norms

There have been few comprehensive attempts to establish norms for handwriting speed at different ages. The guidelines for special arrangements for GCSE examinations recommend that students with a copy-writing speed of 14 words per minute or less should be considered for extra time in order to complete written papers.

Sawyer *et al.* (1992) showed that the average copy-writing speed for a 15-year-old was 25 words per minute.

Cobbett *et al.* (1998) give a mean of 21.6 words per minute for Year 10 students.

Ramsden (unpublished correspondence 1982), using information from his own clinical work, tentatively suggests a mean of 21 words per minute for 15-year-old students. He also suggests similarly tentative means, given below, for the age range 12–18 years.

Considering that word length is an uncontrolled variable in these three studies, there is an interesting concordance between them.

Tentative average age scores suggested by Ramsden's clinical findings:

Age	12	13	14	15	16	17	18
Mean wpm	18	20	20	21	22	22	23
–1 SD	13	15	15	16	17	17	18
–2 SD	8	10	10	11	12	12	13
2/3rd	12	13	13	14	15	15	15

Standard Deviations for all means = 5

2/3rd: This represents the score which is 2/3rd of the average score for the age or worse. It has been suggested that this should be taken as the trigger to request special examination arrangements. At age 15 upwards the 2/3rd is 14 words per minute – the figure selected by the examination boards.

Other surveys have suggested lower means at 15 years, Alston (1995), Connor (1995), Hedderley (1996 cited in Sawyer *et al.* 1992):

	Words per minute		
Age	Alston	Connor	Hedderley
15	16.00		17.00
16	17.00	17.5	20.00
17	18.50		23.00

The variability is perhaps partly due to the fact that word length is an uncontrolled variable in all these studies and partly because of the effects of small population samples. In the absence of reliable norms for words per minute, some clinicians prefer to use letter counts or Sawyer's 0 + 0 test.

Motor Skills Checklist used for the Esteem Clubs

Name: _____

NC Year:_____ DOB: _____

Please rate the child using the 1–5 rating scale where:

High level of skill   1   2   3   4   5   Low level of skill

	1	2	3	4	5
1. Gross-motor activity (games/gym ability)					
2. Fine-motor skills (handwriting)					
3. Coordination (music/dance)					
4. Rhythm (music, skipping)					
5. Basic movement and awareness (can move freely and safely)					
6. Spatial awareness (can complete an obstacle course)					
7. Visual tracking (can intercept a rolling/thrown ball)					
8. Symmetrical activities (skipping, breast-stroke, some gymnastic movements)					
9. Mid-line cross overs (tie knots, dress properly, do up buttons)					
10. Visual sequencing/memory (can play card games)					
11. Visual discrimination and perception (can sort shapes, letters)					
12. Balance – any examples					
13. Auditory sequential memory (can remember 2-3-4 command in sequence, can carry messages)					
14. Auditory discrimination/integrity (Chinese whispers)					
15. Self-esteem (one needs to be mindful of judging the book by the cover)					

Observation Checklists for Motor Skills

1. Patterns of movement may appear 'odd' or different. Closer observation may show:
   Jerky movements
   Making the 'wrong' movement before correction
   Poor fluency and rhythm
   Overlap of movement into opposing limb
   Associated or compensatory movements.
2. Inability to isolate individual body movement with or without verbal command.
3. Inability to coordinate the movements of upper and lower limbs. Increased or decreased muscle tone. Excess effort for executing gross- and fine-motor skills.
4. Inability to start and stop movement appropriately.
5. Difficulty with maintaining a steady balance and posture – standing or sitting.
6. Poor balance skills evident in changing direction, standing on one leg for dressing, PE challenges, bike-riding.
7. Slow to organise tasks and movement.
8. Inability or difficulty copying or reproducing body movements and/or facial expressions.
9. Limited ability to increase speed of movement without disrupting the action or action sequence.
10. Rushing to activities which appears impulsive but may be linked to limited ability to maintain posture and balance when moving.
11. Difficulty moving the body spatially in relation to objects and people when static. More difficulties when the objects and people are moving.
12. Difficulty with estimating speed, direction, distance of movement – whole-body movement and motor skills.

Gross-motor skills

1. Increased tension during movement – this may be most apparent for fine movements.
2. Poor grasp and release.
3. Pincer grip late to develop.
4. Incorrect hand position during tasks.
5. Presence of a tremor – particularly an intention tremor.
6. Continuous mobility of small muscles in the hand.

Fine-motor skills

7. An action and a support hand not established or established late. May swap hands during tasks.
8. Difficulty with crossing the mid-line.
9. Poor bilateral hand skills and poor unilateral hand skills.
10. Difficulty isolating individual finger skills.
11. Poor pencil skills.
12. Poor dressing skills – orientating clothing, sequence of dressing, fastenings, etc.
13. Poor scanning of pictures and text.
14. Jerky eye movements, difficulty crossing the mid-line.
15. Sensitivity to touch.
16. Difficulty mapping point of touch on own body, i.e. poor body awareness.
17. Poor tactile recognition, e.g. when using a feely bag.

References

Alexander, R. (1992) *Policy and Practice in Primary Education*. London: Routledge.

Alston, J. (1995) 'Assessing handwriting speeds: some current norms and issues', *Handwriting Review* **9**.

Ayres, A. J. (1972) *Sensory Integration and Learning Disorders*. Los Angeles: Western Psychological Services.

Baker, L. and Cantwell, D. P. (1987) 'A prospective psychiatric follow-up of children with speech/language disorders', *Journal of the American Academy of Child Psychiatry* **26**, 546–53.

Beery, K. E. (1989) *Developmental Test of Visual Motor Integration*. Cleveland, OH: Modern Curriculum Press.

Bicknell, P. G. and Ripley, K. M. (1987) 'Reading problems and ocular anomalies', *Child Language Teaching and Therapy* **2**, 293–304.

Boivin, M. and Beguin, G. (1989) 'Peer status and self-perception among early elementary school children: The case of rejected children', *Child Development* **60**, 591–6.

Bruce, V. and Young, A. (1986) 'Understanding face recognition', *British Journal of Psychology* **77**, 305–27.

Cartlidge, P. (1995) 'Why do they pick me last?' Unpublished MSc. Thesis, University of Brighton, Sussex.

Chesson, R. *et al.* (1991) 'The consequences of motor/learning difficulties', *Learning* **6**(4).

Clicker 4 Software. *Pre-School and Primary Software Yearbook 2001* REM p. 146.

Cobbett, A. *et al.* (1998) Research Project. UCL MSc Ed. Psychol.

Connor, M. (1995) 'Handwriting performance and GCSE concessions', *Handwriting Review* **9**.

Conrad, K. *et al.* (1984) 'Differentiation of Praxis in children', *American Journal of Occupational Therapy* **37**, 466–73.

Dodge, K. A. (1996) 'A social information processing model of social competence in children', in M. Perlmutter (ed.) *The Minnesota Symposium of Psychology*, 77–125 Hillsdale, NJ: Laurence Erlbaum.

Frost, L. A. and Bondy, A. S. (1994) The Picture Exchange Communication System (PECS). Pyramid Educational Consultants.

Gallahue, D. (1992) *Understanding Motor Development in Children*. London: Wiley.

Gordon, N. and McKinlay, I. (1980) *Helping Clumsy Children*. New York: Churchill Livingstone.

Gordon, N. (1991) 'The relationships between language and behaviour', *Developmental Medicine and Child Neurology* **33**, 86–9.

Greenfield, S. (1998) *The Human Brain*. London: Orion Books.

Gubbay, S. S. (1975) 'The Clumsy Child', in F. C. Rose (ed.) *Pediatric Neurology*, 145–60. Cambridge, MA: Blackwell Scientific.

Hadley, M. and Rice, J. (1991) 'Predictions of interactional failure in preschool children', *Journal of Speech and Hearing Research* **34**, 1308–17.

Henderson, S. E. (1993) 'Motor development and minor handicap', in Kalverboer, A. E. *et al.* (eds) *Motor Development in Early and Late Childhood: Longitudinal Approaches*. Cambridge: Cambridge University Press.

Henderson, S. E. and Hall, D. (1982) 'Concomitants of clumsiness in young school children', *Developmental Medicine and Child Neurology* **24**, 448–60.

Henderson, S. E. and Sugden, D. A. (1992) *Movement Assessment Battery for Children*. Sidcup, Kent: The Psychological Corporation.

Hoare, D. and Larkin, D. (1991) 'Coordination problems in children', *National Sports Research Centre Review* **19**, 1–6.

ICAN (1975) *Language Through Reading Programme*. ICAN Publications.

Kalverboer, A. E. *et al.* (eds) (1993) *Motor Development in Early and late Childhood; Longitudinal Approaches*. Cambridge: Cambridge University Press.

Keogh, J. F. (1968) 'Incidence and severity of awkwardness among regular school boys and educationally subnormal boys', *Research Quarterly* **39**, 806–8.

Keogh, J. F. *et al.* (1979) 'Identification of clumsy children: comparisons and comments', *Journal of Human Movement Studies* **5**, 32–41.

Keogh, J. F. and Sugden, D. A. (1985) *Movement Skill Development*. New York: Macmillan.

La Vigna, G. W. *et al.* (1989) 'The role of positive programming in behavioural treatment', in Cipani, E. (ed.) *Behavioural Approaches to the Treatment of Aberrant Behaviour*. AAMD Monograph Series, Washington DC: American Association on Mental Deficiency.

Lewis, M. and Wray, D. (1995) *Writing Frames*. Exeter Extending Literacy Project.

Losse, A. *et al.* (1991) 'Clumsiness in children – do they grow out of it? A 10 year follow up study', *Developmental Medicine and Child Neurology* **33**, 55–68.

McGrath, M. (1998) 'An Investigation into Poor Coordination and its Implications for Children's Peer Relationships', unpublished MSc thesis, QUB.

Maeland, A. F. (1992) 'Identification of children with motor coordination problems', *Physical Adaptation Quarterly* **9**, 330–42.

Olveus, D. (1978) *Aggression in Schools: Bullies and Whipping Boys*. London: Wiley, Halstead Press.

Orton, S. J. (1937) *Reading, Writing and Speech Problems in Children*. New York: Norton.

Passey, J. (1985) *Cued Articulation and Cued Vowels*. Northumberland: STASS Publications.

Pictures for Projects. SEMERC. *Pre-School & Primary Software Yearbook 2001* REM 86.

Pick, J. P. and Edwards, K. (1997) 'The identification of children with developmental coordination disorder by class and physical education teachers', *British Journal of Educational Psychology* **67**, 55–69.

Polatajko, H. and Fox, A. M. (1995) Children and Clumsiness: A Disability in search of Definition. International Concensus Meeting. London, Ontario, Canada.

Polatajko, H. *et al.* (1995) 'An international consensus on children with developmental coordination disorder', *Canadian Journal of Occupational Therapy* **62**, 3–6.

Ripley, K. M. and Meades, S. (eds) (1988) *Infant Screening Project*. West Sussex LEA.

Ripley, K. M. and Meades, S. (eds) (1998) *Starting Points*. West Sussex LEA.

Ripley, K. M. *et al.* (1997) *Dyspraxia: A Guide for Teachers and Parents*. London: David Fulton Publishers.

Ripley, K. M. *et al.* (2001) *Inclusion for Children with Speech and Language Impairment*. London: David Fulton Publishers.

Russell, J. P. (1988) *Graded Activities for Children with Motor Difficulties*. Cambridge: Cambridge University Press.

Sawyer, C. E. *et al.* (1992) *Educational Psychology in Practice* **8** (2).

Smyth, T. R. and Glencross, D. J. (1986) 'Information processing deficits in clumsy children', *Australian Journal of Psychology* **38**, 13–22.

Spence, S. (1987) 'The Relationship between social-cognitive skills and peer sociometric status', *British Journal of Developmental Psychology* **5**, 347–56.

Stewart, D. (1990) *The Right to Movement – Motor Development in Every School*. London: Falmer Press.

Sugden, D. and Sugden, L. (1991) 'The assessment of movement skills problems in 7–9 year old children', *British Journal of Educational Psychology* **61**, 329–45.

Sugden, D. A. and Keogh, J. F. (1990) *Problems in movement skill development*. Columbia, SC: University of South Carolina.

Walden, T. A. and Field, T. M. (1990) 'Preschool children's social competence and production and discrimination of affective expressions', *British Journal of Developmental Psychology* **8**, 65–76.

Walker, M. (1980) *The Revised Makaton Vocabulary*. St George's Hospital, London: published by the author.

Wechsler, D. (1992) *Wechsler Intelligence Scale for Children* – Third Edition UK. London: The Psychological Corporation.

Wright, H. C. *et al.* (1994) 'Identification of children with movement problems in Singapore: usefulness of the Movement ABC Checklist', *Adapted Physical Activity Quarterly* **11**, 150–7.

Index

Printed in the United Kingdom by
Lightning Source UK Ltd., Milton Keynes
142297UK00010B/3/A

9 781853 467622